Does It Look and Sound Like Jesus?

Cover Photo Courtesy of Bob Burton, Big Canoe, Georgia

Visit www.booksurge.com to order additional copies.

Does It Look and Sound Like Jesus?
Sermons from Big Canoe Chapel

James R. McCormick

Foreword by Maxie Dunnam

2007

Does It Look and Sound Like Jesus?

CONTENTS

To our children, Mark and Lynne, whom I love with a deep father's love, and who are the sources of some of my greatest pride and joy, and...

To the members of Big Canoe Chapel, with whom Patricia and I are privileged to share life and ministry, and whose love, encouragement, and prayer have called forth the best from within me.

FOREWORD

There was a time when Native Americans communicated by drums and smoke signals. Years ago, when the atomic bomb was being tested out on the flats of Nevada, a cartoon pictured some tribesmen. They were looking across the barren wastes...the spacious flats...when on the horizon the mushroom smoke cloud of an atomic explosion rose dramatically. As they looked in wonder...never having seen smoke like this...one said to the other, "I wish I had said that!"

When I hear and/or read my friend Jim McCormick's sermons that is my feeling: I wish I had said that.

Jim is a master preacher. He understands that preaching is more than a mechanical exercise of basic oral communication. It is about communication, but it is both mind and heart reaching out to the minds and hearts of a congregation.

This volume of sermons confirms my assessment. Here is McCormick vintage preaching. Though I'm sure he would hesitate to make the claim, this is his preaching at its best. And what a way to celebrate a congregation's 30th anniversary...a treasury of the essence of what the pastor/preacher has been sharing during his period of leadership.

It is a special joy for me to write this foreword. Jim and I have been friends for nearly fifty years. We shared the same seminary experience. We were young preachers together in Mississippi. We both planted new congregations in our home state. We were both casualties of the civil rights movement and moved to the Southern California-Arizona Conference of the United Methodist Church about the same time in the mid-sixties.

More important than any of that, we believe that preaching is a high calling of God that demands nothing less than all we are and all we can give. Jim has given his best to the art and practical task of preaching. The sermons in this volume witness to the fact that his investment has "paid off" in a marvelous way.

The challenge Jim makes, "Does it Look and Sound Like Jesus?" is a recurring theme in these messages. But he doesn't just challenge us with a question; he offers rich resources to inspire and enable us to look and sound like the One who deserves our ultimate obedience.

Maxie D. Dunnam,
Chancellor, Asbury Theological Seminary

Introduction

This is the 30th Anniversary of the beginning of Big Canoe Chapel. I have been a part of the Chapel's history for almost five years now. Patricia and I had retired and moved to Roswell, Georgia to be near our children and grandchildren. We were happily engaged in a variety of activities common to retired folk when I received a telephone call, asking if I were willing to be considered as an interim pastor of Big Canoe Chapel. To be honest, I had never heard of Big Canoe Chapel, but soon that changed. Following an interview process, I was called to the position. I came to fulfill a three month interim pastorate, and, as I have said, that was almost five years ago. Immediately Patricia and I were captivated by the beauty of the north Georgia mountains. And, shortly after that, we fell in love with the remarkable people of Big Canoe and with their Chapel, and stayed to be in ministry here.

Big Canoe Chapel is a "multi-denominational" congregation. We call it that, rather than "non-denominational" because we are proud to have people of a variety of faith traditions in our membership. And, we don't want people to give up their faith traditions when they become a part of the Chapel; rather, we want them to bring those traditions with them. We respect and embrace them. And we work diligently each day to make the diversity of our faith histories a source of enrichment rather than division. Because we come from a variety of faith traditions, we move to the theological center, and stress those central tenets of the Christian faith that most Christian communities affirm. I believe that the Chapel is a special and distinctive expression of the Christian Church. In very few locations can we worship and serve side by side with so many different kinds of Christians, yet know that we are all one, as a part of God's family. So, I now call myself a "cathobaptoorthometholu palianpresbygationalist"!

Members of the Chapel have been eager to worship and study during the five years I have been their pastor. They have been attentive listeners and informed questioners, and we have grown together. It is a genuine privilege to preach in a congregation like this, and the sermons in this book have grown out of our life together. As we have worshipped and studied and grown together, a recurrent theme has emerged. Now, I can ask a question and be assured of the shared answer. I can ask, "How can we know whether or not something is of God?" Or, "How can we know the extent to which a certain passage of scripture is 'the word of God'?" Or, "How can we know how we are to act in certain circumstances?" The answer will be, "You ask, 'Does it look and sound like Jesus?'"

I think that question is on target, and thus the title of this book, dedicated lovingly to our children, and to the members of Big Canoe Chapel. It is also written with gratitude to Liz Donovan-Davis, who has been immeasurably helpful in publishing this volume of sermons.

1.

By God's Spirit

(The first sermon preached by Dr. McCormick at Big Canoe Chapel)
Zechariah 4:6, Psalms 127:1-2

I believe that God is here. I believe that God wants to meet us here and speak His word of life and give His gift of grace. I really believe in the presence and power of God!

There is no more urgent task confronting the contemporary Church than the intensification of the experience of God at the heart of our life together. Not God as an interesting relic of the past...not God as object of learned discussion...not God as obligatory word uttered and then forgotten...and not God assumed but not central. No, none of that. But God as presence...God as power...God as experienced reality!

Throughout history, whenever the people of God have lost that and have relied only upon their own resources, we have been weak and impotent. But, when we have been sure of God and have sent our roots deep into His greatness, we have been strong.

One of the remarkable stories in the Bible is the story of Gideon. According to the story, God called Gideon to deliver His people by engaging their enemies in battle. But God's instructions to Gideon were unusual to say the least. Gideon was to prepare for battle by reducing his army of 30,000 men down to only 300. And, with that small company of committed men, relying solely upon the strength of God, they won a great victory. Now, the point of the story is that with 30,000 soldiers they might be tempted to rely upon their own strength, thinking that they had no need of God. But with only 300 soldiers, they knew they had to rely upon God, and they learned that such reliance was not misplaced. God was sufficient. God is always sufficient!

So, I repeat: There is no more urgent task confronting the contemporary Church than the intensification of the experience of God at the heart of our life together.

What I am saying may be so obvious to you that it need not be said. Maybe. But, on the other hand, that may be part of the problem: it is so obvious that we are tempted simply to assume it, and by assuming it, we may neglect it. And yet, we dare not neglect that which makes us who we are. What makes us who we are is the experience of that God who has made Himself known to us in Jesus. That experience of God—His grace, His guidance, and His strength—that experience of God is the source of everything good in life. And either that experience is at the heart of our life together, or we are impostors—we are not who we say we are—the people of God!

After all, the Bible begins with it: "In the beginning, God..." The first commandment demands it: "Thou shalt have no other gods before me." The Apostles preached it: "In God we live and move and have our being." Jesus lived it, spending time every day with God in prayer, always pointing past himself to the Father, and always insisting that he could do the remarkable things he did because the Father was with him.

When we have been at our best, we have experienced it too, haven't we? We have known that we are not just talented, sincere, good people trying to do right, but we are God's people, held in His hands, and loved and guided and empowered by His Spirit!

The scripture of the morning goes to the heart of it. Let me share the story with you. Zerubbabel was the governor of Judea in the 6th century B.C. He was a Babylonian Jew who returned to Jerusalem after the Exile to complete the rebuilding of the Temple. The work had been started some 23 years earlier, but it had lost momentum and had come virtually to a stop. There was active opposition from some. And even among those who longed to see the Temple rebuilt, most had lost hope. It was too difficult. It couldn't be done. Then Zerubbabel appeared on the scene and the prophet Zechariah assured the people that Zerubbabel would complete the rebuilding of the Temple. And then he said something very important. Listen: Zerubbabel would be able to complete this difficult task because he was not alone. God was with him. He wasn't dependent only upon his skill and effort, as important as those always are. This is how it would be done: God said, "Not by might, not by power, but by my Spirit." Remember that! What is not possible by human effort alone becomes possible by the power of God's Spirit. I have seen that. I believe that!

We hear that same affirmation in Psalms 127. Listen: "Unless the Lord builds the house, those who build it labor in vain. Unless the Lord watches over the city, the watchman stays awake in vain. It is in vain that you rise up early and go late to rest, eating the bread of anxious toil; for He gives to His beloved in sleep." I particularly like that last thought. As important as human effort is, you don't have to do it all yourself. You are not totally on your own. Even while you are sleeping, God is at work for your good! Isn't that good news?

Do you hear the truth in those words of scripture? You can start early and keep at it until it is late...you can do all you know to do to make yourself healthy, wealthy, wise and happy, but it's not going to work out very well until God is at the center of it, loving, guiding, energizing, empowering.

Listen now, I'm about to say something important. (I always try to give you advance warning!) If I have learned anything in my years of life it is that the whole world is designed to function in a God-centered way. God is to be at the center. And everything else in life is to be ordered around that, deriving its meaning and direction and energy from that vital center. And the fact is, nothing in life is going to work out very well for us until we understand that and begin to cooperate with that.

But when we do, we discover that God is a loving Father who knows how to give good gifts to His children. He is even more anxious to give us good gifts than we are to receive them. We are never alone and on our own. In every experience God is there. In every life situation God is at work for our good. And we can be sure that God's grace is sufficient and God's power is more than adequate!

Read through the pages of history and you will discover that in every generation the Church has seemed to be in trouble. Again and again in history, God's causes have seemed to be lost causes. Look at the very beginning of the Christian movement. Jesus chose 12 disciples. But the record shows that they were slow to learn. Often they were faithless. They quarreled among themselves. And, when the going got tough, they ran away and hid. Not a very likely group with which to start anything significant! But somehow, God's Spirit was at work in their lives, and by God's grace they became the Church. God used that group of ordinary people to do extraordinary things. By the power of God's Spirit, they turned the world upside down! That story has been repeated again and again during the last 20 centuries.

Helmut Thielicke gives us a case in point. Thielicke was a pastor in Germany who graduated from seminary and began his ministry just about the time Adolf Hitler was coming to power. He told about the first prayer meeting he conducted in his first little church. He said he went into that prayer meeting determined to trust in Jesus' words: "All power is given to me in heaven and on earth." He repeated those words to himself again and again, and then went in for the service. Those words were supposed to reassure him that not even Hitler was a match for his Christ. But his entire congregation consisted of two elderly ladies and an even older organist who suffered from palsy. They could hear that, on the outside of the building, there were the marching feet of thousands of Germany's finest youth who had pledged their allegiance to Hitler. The contrast could not have been more dramatic. Thielicke remembered thinking to himself, "Is this all you have to set before me, Jesus, you to whom all power has been given, or supposedly given? Jesus, haven't you been utterly repudiated by what is happening in Germany today?"

So it would seem. But now, only a few short years later, Adolf Hitler has gone down the drain of history, and here we are gathered in this Chapel as the Church, to sing our hymns, pray our prayers, and affirm our faith. Don't you ever underestimate what God can do!

Just think about the history of this Chapel. It's impressive by any standard of measurement. The buildings built…the classes taught…the prayers prayed…the lives touched and made new by Christ…the many helping ministries: scholarships provided, tutoring done, the needy helped, the hurting encouraged, the grieving comforted, and so many missions staffed and funded. Where would the list end? I look at all of that and I can only say, "Wow!"

But even as you have been doing all of that, I am sure there have been those crossroads moments when there have been doubts and fears and questions. I am sure there have been times when the resources, both human and financial, have seemed inadequate for the task to be done. But God never abandons His people. And again and again, His power has seen us through. And He isn't through with us yet!

As we move into the future, it is important to remember that the history of the Chapel is not just the story of what has been accomplished by intelligent, talented, generous, and hard-working people. That's only part of the story. Primarily, the history of the Chapel is the story of what God has done in and through the lives of people who have made themselves available to Him. That's the way it always happens: "Not by might, nor by power, but by God's Spirit."

I want you to know that I am excited about the future of this congregation. I believe that the best days are not in our past but in our future. I believe that when we are open to it, God gives us dreams of what can be, calls us to give ourselves to make those dreams come true, and then works in our lives to provide all that we need.

But I warn you, when God gives us a dream, it is a God-sized dream, requiring nothing less than our best. So, during my time here, I will be asking you to stretch and strain and grow and reach out, giving of your very best. But I won't apologize for that. I will glory in it because anything less would not be faithful to the gospel. I don't know about you, but I couldn't get too excited about a God who asks only for our leftovers. I couldn't be motivated by a God who is willing to settle for mediocrity. No, the thing that excites and motivates me is precisely that God asks for our best! And He gives us tasks of such size and significance that nothing less than our best will do!

Now hear me: the good news is that we don't have to be afraid of God's big dreams, because we worship a big God who is able to assure big results. That's why I don't fear the future with all its uncertainty. Because the most important thing is certain: the same God who has loved and guided and sustained and strengthened us in the past will accompany us into that future. Even while we sleep, God will be at work for our good.

My favorite hymn says it: "Through many dangers, toils, and snares we have already come. 'Tis grace has brought us safe thus far, and grace will lead us home." I believe that. I trust that!

In closing, let me give you a vision of the future. I borrow it from "Star Trek." Have you ever listened carefully to the words with which every episode of "Star Trek" begins? Listen: "This is the story of the star ship 'Enterprise,' on its mission to new worlds, to seek out new life, and boldly to go where no one has ever gone before." Listen to that from the Christian perspective and see if you can hear a God-sized dream in it:

> To be on mission to new worlds—to seek out new life—and boldly to go where no one has ever gone before.

I tell you, I could get excited about a dream like that! Of course, it's frightening. It's difficult. There will always be people around us saying, "It's too expensive. It's impossible. You can't do it!"

But, remembering who we are, remembering whose we are, and remembering how far God's grace and power have already brought us, as always the people of God will answer: "By God we can, too! By God—we can!"

"Not by might, nor by power, but by my Spirit, says the Lord."

Prayer: For all that has been, we give you thanks, our Father. For all that will yet be by Your grace and power, we commit our lives to You anew. Work in us and through us to do Your will. In the name of Christ we pray. Amen.

2.
Follow Me!

Matthew 16:21-25

It was the beginning of new life for Peter and Andrew on that day, by the Sea of Galilee, when Jesus tapped them on the shoulder and said, "Come, follow me." And, what an opportunity he gave to Matthew, the tax collector, when he issued the invitation to him, "Matthew, come, follow me." Those three, and the other nine disciples all answered, "Yes." But there were others who heard the call and said, "No." There were those balking inquirers who responded with excuses, "I've just gotten married," or "Let me go and bury my father." And, there was the one we call "the rich young ruler." Jesus told him to go and sell all that he had and give it to the poor, and then come and follow me. The scriptures say that he went away sorrowful, also answering, "No."

So, Jesus gave them and Jesus gives us the freedom to decide. But, my, how much is at stake in answering that question: "Will you follow me?" In the first century, those who decided to follow Jesus became disciples. By that we mean that they lived with Jesus, listened to Jesus, learned from Jesus. They followed him wherever he went. Their lives were changed as a result. And then, as Jesus' earthly life was coming to its end—as he could see the rejection, the persecution and the death that awaited him in Jerusalem—he felt the need to put the question to them again. Were they still willing to follow him? He said, "If any want to be my followers, let them deny themselves, and take up their cross, and follow me." They had to decide all over again: "Is this really what you want? Are you willing to pay the price of discipleship?"

Let's look carefully at what Jesus said to them, and what Jesus says to us.

I.

First, he said, if you want to be my disciple, you must deny yourself. Deny yourself—that doesn't mean what a lot of people think it means. It doesn't mean to put yourself down, devalue yourself, deny yourself all pleasures and all good experiences in life. No, not that. Jesus said that he came to give us life, not to take it away.

Where did we get the idea that God wants us to put ourselves down—refuse to affirm ourselves as persons of worth? To deny yourself does not require demeaning ourselves. No, when Jesus says, "Deny yourself," he is saying, "Do not put yourself at the center of life. That's where God belongs." Jesus is saying, "Take yourself off the throne of life, and allow God to take His rightful place there."

Clearly, in the gospels we are not told to put ourselves down. Listen, we are the sons and daughters of God, created in His image. We don't always act like it, but that is who we are. So, we are to love ourselves. Jesus did not say, "Love your neighbor instead of yourself." He said, "Love your neighbor as you love yourself." Psychologists agree that we cannot love others in healthy ways unless we first love ourselves in healthy ways. So, the problem is not self love. Be clear about that. The problem is self centeredness.

That was the central theme of Jesus' teaching. Jesus talked repeatedly about the Kingdom of God. What he was saying is that God is to be at the center of life; God is to be the anchor that holds everything else in its proper place. The whole world is designed to function with God at its center, so when you put yourself or anyone or anything else there, it all goes wrong. You want to mess up your life? Put yourself at the center of it. You want to miss out on the best in life? Put yourself at the center. Only God will do. That's what Jesus was getting at when he said, "Seek first the Kingdom of God (that is, the God centered life—seek that first) then everything else that you need will be yours as well."

That's what Jesus did. The Kingdom was first in his life. God was at the center of his life. So, if we want to follow him, to be his disciples, we must deny ourselves first place, and allow God to have first place. And when we do, then everything will fit together and life will be what it is intended to be. That's the first thing—deny yourself.

II.

The second thing Jesus said about being his disciple is that we must take up our cross. That's the disturbing thing about the cross—Jesus is not the only one who gets one. As the gospel song asks: "Must Jesus bear the cross alone, and all the world go free? No, there's a cross for everyone, and there's a cross for me." But again, taking up our cross does not mean what many people think it means.

All my life I've heard people who were ill, or who had experienced something painful or disappointing say, "Well, I guess this is just my cross, and I have to bear it." But they are wrong. The cross is not something difficult or painful that comes to us involuntarily. That's not what happened to Jesus. Remember, Jesus said, "No one takes my life from me. I lay it down." Jesus went voluntarily to the cross out of obedience to God.

That was what the struggle in the Garden of Gethsemane was about. Jesus did not want to die. He could see the cross looming before him, and he did not want to die—not then, so early in his life—and not like that—so painful, so lonely, so rejected. The struggle was so intense that sweat appeared on his brow like great drops of blood. But, finally, he received the grace necessary to pray the greatest prayer that can be prayed. He prayed, "Not my will, but Thine be done."

So, the cross we are called to bear is the same as the cross Jesus was called to bear. The cross is the cross of obedience. Hear that: the cross of obedience...the willingness and the ability to pray, "Not my will, but Thine be done."

My, that's difficult. Again and again I have had people tell me that the single most difficult thing about being a disciple is giving up control. We want to decide what commandments we will obey and which we will not. We want to decide whom we will love and under what circumstances we will serve. We want a God we can veto when the going gets tough or when the price gets too high. Well, we are right back at the beginning, aren't we? We have just taken God off the throne and put ourselves back on. When we refuse to take up the cross of obedience, we are also refusing to deny ourselves first place. I'm in charge!

To give up control is not easy. But when we come to know that God is like Jesus, that He really loves us and cares about us, then we can trust that He knows what is best for us and that He wants what is best for us. Once we know that, really know that, then we can pray and mean, "Not my will, but Thine be done." Jesus says, "Take up your cross—the cross of obedience." That's the second thing.

III.

Then, Jesus says, "Come, follow me." I don't know of any more important decision in life than the decision about whom to follow. Because, the destination we reach is determined by the road we take. Certainly we want a guide who knows the way!

I have seen T-shirts, and probably you have too, that bear the imprint, "Don't follow me. I'm lost!" At least they are honest. Jesus warned about the blind following the blind. He said that the inevitable result will be that both will fall into the ditch. One of the saddest things in life is to decide to follow someone—we follow, follow, follow—and then late in life we discover that the one we have followed has not taken us where we really wanted to go. How sad!

Every one of us wants the very best in life, I'm sure of that. We don't want any good thing to pass us by. We want our lives to count for something. We want the world to know that we were here. We don't want to come to the end of our lives and have to admit that we have missed it; we have blown it. So, the decision about whom to follow is an important one indeed.

Jesus called his first century disciples and he calls us, saying, "Come, follow me." The question of all questions is, "Does he know where he is going? Is that where I want to go, too?" That's important because who you follow not only determines where you go, it also profoundly shapes what you experience and who you become along the way. Jesus' first century disciples lived with Jesus, listened to Jesus, learned from Jesus. And, day by day, something of Jesus' spirit began to be imprinted upon them. They began to see with the eyes of Jesus. They began to feel and care with the heart of Jesus. They began to reach out compassionately with the hands of Jesus. Over time, they began to look and sound like Jesus. And, they turned the world upside down.

You remember that, toward the end of Jesus' life, he became aware that most people had rejected him. Thousands had heard him teach, and most of them said, "No." How sad. All Jesus wanted to do was to love them. All he wanted to do was to bring them to the Father. All he wanted to do was to give them life at its best, and to help them make the world a better place for all God's children. But, most of them listened, and then walked away. So, Jesus asked his disciples, "Will you also go away?" I love what Peter said in response. He said, "Lord, to whom shall we go? You have the words of eternal life!"

That's what I have decided as well. Of all the choices available to me in life, I have decided that the best choice is to follow Jesus. I don't know of a better picture of God than the one I see in Jesus. I don't know of a more authentic and attractive model of human life than the one I see in Jesus. I don't know of a better way for us to live with one another than the compassionate, serving, self-giving life modeled by Jesus. There is nothing that takes hold of me in the deep places of my life, challenges me, and calls forth the best from within me as does all of that that I see in Jesus.

It's true! In the company of Jesus I see things I have never seen before. I dream dreams I have never dreamed before. I am challenged to do life-giving things I have never done before. I become more than I have ever been before. Where else can we go? Jesus has the words of eternal life, and he is the way. I'm sure of it. So, I have decided to follow him.

Of course, it's not always easy. Following Jesus does lead to a cross, you know. But, Jesus never said it was easy. Remember the man who said to Jesus, "Lord, I will follow you wherever you go." Jesus cautioned him, "The foxes have holes, and the birds have their nests, but I don't even have a place to lay my head." Are you sure? No, he did not say it would be easy. But he did promise to be with us. He did promise to give us everything we need for the journey. And he promised that following him will lead to abundant life, eternal life.

We keep saying it over and over again don't we? One of things I'm most pleased about is that phrase that's become an important part of our lexicon. In every class and in every sermon, I can ask, "How do we know when it is God? How do we know how we should act?" And, in unison the answer always comes back, "Does it look and sound like Jesus?" I'm pleased about that, because, that's what it means. To follow Jesus means that, over time, by keeping company with him, by opening ourselves to him, we begin to look and sound like him. And when we do, we become "the body of Christ," we become the best we will ever be, and life becomes the best it can be.

Two examples: Ernest Campbell once told about the time when he was pastor in Ann Arbor, Michigan. Shortly after the assassination of President Kennedy, the whole country was in shock and grief. A member of that congregation came to Reverend Campbell and suggested that one redemptive thing they might do would be to bring Marina Oswald to Ann Arbor, provide a place for her to live, and help her to improve her English. (She had said that she wanted to stay in the U.S.A. and to improve her English.)

So, they brought her to Ann Arbor, quietly and without fanfare. They moved her in with a loving family, and began to be of any help they could. When word of their actions began to get out, the reaction was swift and angry. Critics said that their action was unwise, unfair, unpatriotic, and even un-American. Patiently, Reverend Campbell answered every criticism by letter. And to every critic he said the same thing: "The one thing you haven't shown us is that what we have done is unlike Jesus." There's that question again, "Does it look and sound like Jesus?" Jesus got into trouble for the same thing. He loved the unlovely and welcomed the outcasts. And they killed him for it.

It happened to me. I was sitting at my desk one day when I received a telephone call. A husky voice asked, "Can I come to your church?" It was such a strange question that I asked the caller why he had asked it. He explained that he was a Marine, a Vietnam veteran, and that for years he had felt like a woman trapped in a man's body. He was saving his money for an operation. But, in the meanwhile, he had let his hair grow long and he was dressing and living as a woman. That's why he wanted to know if he could come to our church. Privately I wished that he had called someone else, but what could I do? It's not my church or your church. It is Christ's church. And he welcomed everybody. So, I told him, of course, he could come.

Well, Mike or Michelle, as he had begun to call himself, came the next Sunday morning. And, I have to say, lovingly, that he looked like a burly Marine dressed in women's clothes. He stood out. When he walked down for communion, he wobbled in high heels. And, it was not a one time experience; he came Sunday morning, and Sunday night, and Wednesday night. And, bless their hearts, I am so proud of the members of that congregation, especially some of the older women. They invited Michelle to sit with them. They accepted him just as he was. And he kept coming—I am sure that at least one reason was that the church was the only place in the world where he was loved and accepted just as he was.

But, some were uncomfortable—I was uncomfortable—it's not the kind of thing you encounter every day. And there was talk—"Where does he go to the rest room? What are we to tell our children?" And there were threats—"We won't be back as long as Michelle's here." It came to a head one night in a Bible study class. All the questions, all the concerns. Finally, I went to the white board and with marker in hand, I said, "I understand the discomfort. I really do. So, help me to write an invitation to the church, in the name of Jesus, that will allow me to tell Michelle that he is unwelcome here." Silence. A long, pregnant silence. They had come to know something about Jesus. And not a single member of that congregation was willing to say, "You're not welcome here."

It's not always easy. To follow Jesus—to live a life that looks and sounds like Jesus—it's not easy. But it's the hope of the world. And it's the best hope of your life and mine.

"If any want to be my followers, let them deny themselves and take up their cross and follow me." That's what he said!

Last spring, when some of us renewed our baptisms at the Jordan River in Israel, we sang, "I have decided to follow Jesus." It was a deeply moving time for us as we renewed our commitment to be his disciples. Let's remember the words and make them our own: "I have decided to follow Jesus—no turning back, no turning back."

Prayer: Thank you Father for claiming us as Your own and calling us to follow Jesus. Help us to recognize him as the way, the truth, and the life. Help us so to live with him and to learn from him that we begin to look and sound like him. In Jesus' name we pray. Amen.

3.
Make Room for Mystery

Isaiah 55:8-9

There is a poem which begins: "God moves in a mysterious way, His wonders to perform." There was a time in history when people were quite comfortable with that idea. After all, for pre-scientific people, the mysterious, the unexplainable was a part of everyday life. There was so much that they could not understand that they put it all in the general category of "mystery," and they accounted for that by pointing to God. If they couldn't understand it, they simply said, "God did it!"

They couldn't begin to explain night and day, the coming of the seasons, why a seed when placed in the earth will germinate, sprout, and grow to a full plant when the process begins again. They couldn't understand why rain falls, why winds blow, what makes the tides of the ocean. Human birth was a mystery, of course. I could go on and on. There was so much about life that they could not explain. But they cooperated with the processes of life. They used even that which they could not understand. And they simply said about all of that, "God does it!"

Then came the education explosion. The printing press was invented and the common people began to read. More and more people went to school. The scientific revolution came. Science began to explain more and more of the things that had been unexplainable. The horizons of human knowledge were expanded again and again. Today, we can understand so much about life, that many people assume that we can understand everything. For many of our contemporaries there is no longer any room for mystery, not even any room for God.

I.

We are living at a time in history when great emphasis is placed upon the rational. We have great confidence in the ability of the human mind to understand life and the world in which we live. And, I am proud to say, the Christian Church has had a major role in the development of human knowledge. The first great universities in this country were founded by the Christian Church. We Christians have long proclaimed that God gave us minds and He expects us to use them. We have understood that a major part of our purpose in life is to search for the truth, wherever that truth is to be found, because all truth is God's truth, and wherever you find truth, you find God. I believe that. I believe that deeply! So, hear me loud and clear: there is no excuse for fuzzy thinking. The failure to develop our minds is poor stewardship of a God given gift.

In the Christian tradition in which I was raised, there was a two-fold emphasis: the warm heart and the enlightened mind. I am proud of that. I am proud to be a part of a Church that does not ask you to park your brain before coming to worship. I am sure that God expects us to use our minds to their fullest capacity!

But there is a two-fold problem. First, there are Christians who wrongly think that God is pleased the more irrational things we can believe in the name of faith. No, God is not honored by a mind numbing, irrational picture of the gospel. We cannot affirm that. And, second, there are those who are overly impressed with what our minds can do. They believe that, given time, there is nothing we cannot understand, categorize, and quantify. Everything in life that does not fit established rational categories is simply dismissed. So, instead of using our minds to enlarge our experience of life, for such people life itself is reduced to the size of our minds. Tragically, many people have become convinced that if we can't touch it, it isn't real, and if we can't understand it, it isn't important. Clearly, a person with this picture of life has no room in his world for wonder, or awe, or reverence. There is no room for mystery.

Now, all of this is particularly difficult at Christmas. Because when we read the Christmas story, we read about guiding stars, angelic choirs, virgin births, and a baby in a manger splitting history in two. The temptation for us moderns is to dismiss it all as some kind of fairy tale because we have no rational category in which to place it all. But, if we yield to that temptation, and try to make Christmas something which is totally rational and understandable—if we remove the mystery, and reduce the incarnation to the size of our minds, we will have lost something essential.

II.

And here's why: there is more to life than the rational dimension. In all life, and certainly in all authentic religion, there is a mystery which goes beyond reason. Now, please understand that when I use the term, "mystery," I am not talking about something which is irrational, contrary to reason, but something which is supra-rational, going beyond reason. I have no respect for that kind of religion which seems to say that the more irrational things you can believe, the more favor you gain with God. No, not that. We want to be guided by reason as far as sound reason can take us. But there is a dimension to life which goes beyond reason. There are ways of understanding life which are not purely rational.

Throughout history, the greatest thinkers were humbled by the realization of how little they really knew. The more they learned, the more they discovered they did not know. So, they tended to approach life with a sense of reverence and wonder. Albert Einstein, no small intellect, possessed a kind of reverent humility. He once said, "The most beautiful thing we can experience is the mysterious, the sense of wonder in the presence of something partly known and partly hidden. The one to whom this emotion is a stranger, who can no longer stand wrapped in awe and wonder, is as good as dead, a snuffed out candle." I am impressed with the fact that this brilliant scientist, who understood so much, still made room in his life for mystery.

The ancient Hebrews had a real sense of the mysterious. For example, they would not even pronounce the name, "Yahweh," because that was God's name, and it was holy. In the center of the Temple was the "Holy of holies," the dwelling place of God. No one entered there except for the High Priest, and that was only once each year. For them, God was the "other," the holy, the mysterious. They probably carried that a bit too far. But they were nearer right than those of us who no longer have room for mystery.

I like to think of myself as a well-educated, intelligent, rational person. Whatever is, I want to know about it and to understand it. And, for someone, even for me, to suggest that there are parts of life I will never fully understand makes me very uncomfortable. I have been programmed to believe that talk of mystery, things beyond our understanding, is really an intellectual cop-out. I recoil when I hear people say too quickly, "Well, there are just some things we're not supposed to understand." That's one reason I am preaching this sermon. Periodically I need to wrestle with those things that make me uncomfortable so that I can grow. So, this sermon is for me. I am saying some things that I need to hear. And, if you like, I'll let you listen in to what I am saying to me.

What I am pleading for is a balance to life. We must ask and answer as many questions as we can. We must never stop searching for the truth. But, once we have reached the end of our mind's leash, we must acknowledge that there is more to life than what we understand. As God has said, "My thoughts are not your thoughts, nor are your ways my ways." After we have wrestled with the great issues of life, there will always be an appropriate time to kneel in reverence and humility before that which is mystery.

H.G. Wells dealt with it in his story, "The Soul of a Bishop." In the story, there is a conversation between the Bishop and an angel. The angel is telling him that all religions are trying to express a truth which they don't clearly know, a mystical something that eludes the mind as water escapes the hand. The Bishop said, hoping for an exclusive revelation, "But, the truth, you can tell me the truth." The angel smiled, cupped his hand over the Bishop's bald spot, stroked it affectionately, and then held his head firmly in his hands while he said, "Truth! Yes, I could tell you. But could this hold it? Not this little box of brains. You haven't things to hold it with inside this." It's true, isn't it? There is much in life that we can understand. But there is much that we can't. Mystery.

Isn't it true that at the deepest levels of our human experience we are always out of the reach of satisfactory explanations? We can't explain how we are moved to tears by a great play or a magnificent piece of music. When a great artist produces a painting, he doesn't attempt to explain it—it is to be experienced, not explained. How can we account for the goose bumps when we look up into a starry sky, or when we watch the sun go down in glory behind the mountains? How can you explain the sense of wonder when your life is touched by God? And what about the overwhelming experiences of human love? Can we really put those into words, or explain them in any satisfactory way?

Robert Burns once wrote, "O my luve's like a red, red rose, that's newly sprung in June." Now, as a factual statement, that's ridiculous. There is a great deal of difference between a rose and a human being. But Burns was not trying to make a statement of objective fact. He was trying to share an experience. By means of a poetic picture, he was attempting to get at a mystery...the mystery of love.

I am convinced that the deepest levels of human experience are dealt with best not by analysts—not by detached, objective, rational reporters, but by people who get inside of an experience, and seek to share that experience, even though they know they cannot adequately explain it. The deepest things in life cannot be fully described...they can only be hinted at. They cannot be looked at directly, but obliquely. That's why it takes artists, and poets, and musicians to deal with the deep things of life, because they have the sensitivity necessary to deal with mystery.

I suppose that's why I have never seen a totally satisfying movie about Jesus. Whenever I have seen Jesus depicted on the screen, usually he has come across to me as just another human being—a rather nice human being, with a bag of tricks perhaps, but just another human being. You look at him that directly and you miss the experience of the divine that was at work in him. You miss the mystery. That's why the oblique look is required. I experience Jesus much more authentically in Handel's "Messiah" than in any movie I have ever seen. Maybe—maybe that's why the Bible is much more closely akin to poetry than to biography. The Bible probes the depths of life, while making room for transcendence and mystery.

You can understand, then, why guiding stars and angelic choirs are essential parts of the Christmas story. How can you express that which is inexpressible, that which is supra-rational, unless you talk of such things?

There will always be mystery involved in authentic religion. If there is a God at all, He will always be beyond our understanding. That's why you have heard me say, "We can never say completely what God is— we can only say what God is at least." For that God to express Himself uniquely in a baby born in a manger boggles the mind. And for there to be a power at work in that baby that has touched millions of lives and made them new is something I cannot fully understand. I don't know about you, but I don't want to make the Incarnation sound like the simplest and most natural thing in the world. I don't want to reduce the Christian gospel to something so innocuous that no leap of faith is required to believe it. The Apostle Paul insisted that the gospel is a scandal, a folly, a stumbling block to the "worldly wise." No matter how you slice it, there is a mystery to the gospel which does not rest easily on our minds! Mystery!

Listen now, because I'm about to say something important: increasingly, I am becoming more comfortable with mystery. I'm becoming more comfortable saying that there is much in the Christian gospel I do not fully understand. And the reason for that is this: I deeply believe that God is like Jesus. The way we know about God's presence and about God's action is to ask, "Does it look and sound like Jesus?" Because I believe that is true, I also believe that the part of God and the part of life that I do not fully understand is not unlike that which I do understand. That means it is like Jesus…and that means, finally, it is good.

There will always be mystery in authentic religion. But I don't apologize for that, I glory in it. Because if I could fully understand the Christian faith, if I could fully understand God with my little box of brains, there would be nothing about the gospel big enough or powerful enough to do what I need!

Down deep, don't we all sense the truth of that? In the depths of our lives, don't we all long for some experience of that which is beyond our comprehension? Don't we all long for an experience of the transcendent God, who "moves in a mysterious way, His wonders to perform?"

III.

Wouldn't it be great if we could recover our lost sense of wonder? Wouldn't it be great if we could look at life with the eyes of the spirit and see the hand of God at work everywhere? If we could experience life like that we would want to break into poetry or into song—or at the very least to stand in silent reverence before the magnificent and mysterious works of God.

Jesus said that before we can do that, we must become like children. Have you ever noticed that for little children nothing is commonplace? Nothing is dull and routine. Everything has a freshness and excitement about it. Jesus said that's the way to do it. We must approach life with a gleam in our eye, with a look of wonder on our face, and we've got to experience it all with unrestrained excitement.

Well, isn't that the feeling you get when you hear the Christmas story? Something was happening—something so significant that angelic choirs sang about it and a star moved across the sky to point to where it was happening. The shepherds did not fully understand what was happening, but they knew it was important, and they responded by kneeling before the manger in reverence and wonder.

Note those words: reverence and wonder. Is that the way you would respond? I fear that many of us would be content to snap pictures, take notes, and try to understand it all. The shepherds simply knelt before the manger in reverence and wonder. And if we have become so sophisticated that we have lost our capacity for that, we have lost something essential.

Listen! The good news of the gospel is that "the Word became flesh and lived among us, full of grace and truth.". I don't fully understand that. I try, but I really don't. But that's okay, because I have experienced that. And believe me, the experience of it is far better than the understanding. A poet said it like this:

"I know not how that Bethlehem's Babe could in the God-head be;
I only know the manger child has brought God's life to me.
I know not how that Calvary's cross a world from sin could free;
I only know its matchless love has brought God's love to me."

I've experienced that.

O, if you are intellectually curious, and I hope you are, you are welcome to investigate the records. Christianity is an historic religion and there is much factual data. I'll be happy to discuss the faith with you at length. We can intellectualize for hours. I'll go with you as far as reason can take us. We ought to do that, because it's important.

I want to live in that kind of rational world. I want to do my intellectual homework. But I hope you will understand when I say that I also want to live in a spiritual and emotional world in which I can hear angelic choirs and see stars pointing me to Christ. I want to open my mind. But I also want to open my heart and my imagination to the mystery all around me, so that when you look for me at Christmas, you will find me with the shepherds, kneeling before the manger in reverence and wonder.

There is mystery in life, you know. I can't fully understand it, but I can name it. The name of it is God.

A prayer by Ernest Campbell:

Lord, we know the words,
Teach us now the music of our faith.
We know the forms of celebration,
Give us now the fire, the passion, and the joy.
Break through the curtain of our dark,
And help us to receive You unashamed,
With the abandon of a little child.
In the Savior's name we pray. Amen.

4.
It's Good News!

I John 4:9-10

Recently we observed the one hundredth anniversary of the Wright brothers first flight in an airplane. One hundred years ago, when news of the flight began to spread, a disbelieving cynic said, "I don't believe it. Nobody's ever going to fly. But if they do, it won't be anybody from Dayton, Ohio!"

We do tend to be skeptical about good news, don't we, and particularly so when the alleged good news comes from an unlikely source. One hundred years ago it was difficult enough to believe that people could fly. But surely, if such a remarkable event were to take place, it would involve some important people from New York City or from one of the other leading cities of the world; but a couple of preacher's kids from Dayton, Ohio? No way!

Similarly, in the first century it was difficult enough to believe in God. It was even more difficult to believe that God would love his people enough to act in history to deliver them. But to believe that such a cosmic event would take place in the obscure, out-of-the-way, unimportant village of Bethlehem—that's just too much!

And it really stretches our imagination when we add the other factors: Mary and Joseph were poor. They were Jews and the Jews were a conquered people. They had no influence, prestige, or power. They were nobodies, really. Add all those factors together and you will have to agree that this was not the time, the place, nor the manner in which God would be expected to act.

Suppose you had been outside the stable in Bethlehem on that first Christmas night. Would you have expected anything significant to be happening there? Of course not. Everything important happened in Rome, or in Athens, or at least in Jerusalem. And it involved the rich, the educated, or the powerful. What could you expect from a group of poor nobodies in a barn?

Christopher Fry has expressed the same feelings in poetry:

"The darkest time in the year,
The poorest place in the town,
Cold, and a taste of fear,
Man and woman alone,
What can we hope for here?"

At first glance, that is how we would summarize the situation. A man and a woman in a barn—no hope there, no great expectations there! That's the way it looks when we leave God out of the picture. But add God to that scene, a God determined to reveal Himself to His people, to act for the salvation of His people—add God to the picture and it changes dramatically. Because when God enters that scene it is changed from an ordinary, uneventful, even hopeless situation into the incarnation, the gospel, good news for the entire world. Listen as Christopher Fry continues his poem:

"What can we hope for here?
More light than we can learn,
More wealth than we can treasure,
More love than we can earn,
More peace than we can measure,
Because one child is born."

There are no words large enough to express what the birth of that child has meant to the world. We've been trying to say it for 2000 years now—in books, drama, poetry, and art. And we still haven't found a canvas large enough to portray it. Of course, this child was not just any child. Jesus was a child in whom God was uniquely present. In him God acted to reveal Himself. In him God acted to bring about reconciliation between Himself and all people everywhere.

The story of that event—the story of the life, death, and resurrection of Jesus, and what it means to us is called the gospel, or, the good news. When we understand it, when we experience it, and when we receive it in faith, we know that there is no other way to say it: it is good news indeed!

George Kaufman, the playwright, once said that he began life as an optimist, but he got over it. He said that often, when the telephone rang, he would rush to it, hoping that it would be good news. But usually it was someone asking for a loan, or asking him to help a relative get a job. He said, "It took me a long time to realize that people were not sitting around saying, 'What good thing, what wonderful thing can we do for George Kaufman? Let's call him and tell him about it.'" No one was doing that.

That is, no one but God. Don't you see, that's precisely what Christmas is about. And that is why it is such good news. God has something good to give us: Himself—His love—His forgiveness—His gift of abundant life. He gave us all of that, and more, when He gave us the gift of Jesus at Christmas. That's why we sing, "Joy to the world, the Lord is come!" The message of Christmas is good news!

I.

Part of the good news is the impact that Jesus' birth has had upon the world. The world has been dramatically flavored by the salt of Christ. The world has been illumined by the light of Christ. All of life is dramatically different because of His entrance into human history.

Usually when a person dies, his influence gradually wanes. Like dropping a pebble into a pond, the ripples, quite noticeable at the point of impact, gradually diminish and then disappear. But with Jesus, just the opposite took place. He was little known throughout the world just following his death and resurrection. But today, twenty centuries later, his influence goes far beyond our ability to express.

I think about that man who was lukewarm, if not indifferent, about Christian missions, that is, until he took a trip around the world and saw first-hand the impact of Jesus' life. He returned an enthusiastic spokesman for Christian missions. His name is Henry Van Dusen, and he wrote a book entitled, "For the Healing of the Nations." He made a startling claim in his book. He claimed that no one had to tell him when he left a village where Christ was not known and entered one in which Christ was known. He said that he could see the difference by looking at the people, observing their behavior, sensing their spirit.

That rings true in our experience, doesn't it? We know from our experience that that sort of thing always happens among people when God is given a chance at our lives.

It is certainly true in my life that the highest values I know have come from Christ: justice, mercy, compassion, forgiveness, and love. His influence has not waned; even after 2000 years, his light still shines. His salt still flavors our lives. His leaven is still at work in our world. So many human problems have been solved and so many other problems will yet be solved by a rebirth of his spirit in the world. It's true: our lives have been immeasurably enriched and blessed because he came. Christmas is good news!

II.

We have been talking about the world-wide impact of Jesus' birth. Now let's talk for a few moments about the personal impact. God has come to us in Jesus to do for every one of us that which we cannot do for ourselves. Don't ever forget that. God took the initiative. God took the first step.

Please understand, once and for all, that the Christian gospel always starts with God and not with us. The initiative is His. Listen to this emphasis in scripture: "By grace you have been saved through faith. It is not your own doing. It is the gift of God." "While we were still sinners, Christ died for us." "This is love, not that we loved God, but that He loved us, and sent His Son for our sins." Over and over again in the gospels, God is pictured as the good shepherd who goes out in search of the one sheep that is lost.

We keep turning that around, picturing us as the shepherd, looking for God as if He is lost. But that's all wrong. Hear me: we will never understand the Christian gospel until we understand that it is not a discovery we have dug up in some library. It is not something we have invented by our genius. It is not something we have conjured up in our imagination. The gospel did not originate with us. It is a gift from God! It is the gift of Himself: His love, His mercy, His forgiveness, and His gift of abundant life.

Surely that is the heart of the gospel—God giving Himself to us in Jesus! We hear the echoes of it again and again in the gospels. Jesus says, "He who has seen me has seen the Father." The gospel of John says: "The Word became flesh and lived among us, full of grace and truth." Even the name for Jesus, given to Mary by the angel, the name "Emmanuel" says it. "Emmanuel" means "God with us." That's the heart of it, isn't it? In Jesus, God came to us, revealed Himself to us, and by His amazing grace, reconciled us to Himself, and enabled us to live as His sons and daughters.

You know, the more I grow in my experience of the gospel, the more I see the divine wisdom in God's acting as He did. When God decided to reveal Himself in human flesh, and when all had been prepared, He did not come as a giant, as Joseph Fort Newton has said, "stalking up and down the earth, terrifying the little folk out of their wits." Instead He decided to reach out to us as "a little child, and let earthborn creatures hold Him in their arms." Or, as Paul Scherer expressed it so beautifully, "God just walked down the staircase of heaven with a baby in His arms."

That tells you something about God, doesn't it? It tells you about divine tenderness, gentleness, and sensitivity. I remember the story of a mother reading the Bible to her little daughter. She read John 3:16: "For God loved the world so much that He gave His only Son, that whoever believes in Him shall not perish, but have eternal life." The mother turned to her daughter and said, "Isn't that wonderful?" The daughter said, "No." The mother was upset. She read the verse a second time and then asked again, "Isn't that wonderful?" The little girl said, matter of factly, "Why no, mother. It would be wonderful if it were anyone else, but it's really just like God."

I think they both were right. It is wonderful, and it really is just like God. It's just like God to love us when we are so unlovely. It's just like God to seek us when we go astray. It's just like God, in Jesus, to die upon a cross to save us when we cannot save ourselves. It's just like God! And that's exactly what is good about the good news!

I can't tell you how reassuring it is to me to know that there is nothing I can do to make God stop loving me. And there is nothing I can do to make God love me more than He already does. God's love is constant, unwavering, and unconditional!

Underline that! The good news of the gospel is not how we feel about God, but how God feels about us, not that we love God, but that God loves us. We have to receive that gift in faith. We have to trust it. We have to live as if it is true. But the place where it all starts is with God's love made known to us in Jesus. As our scripture puts it: "This is love: not that we love God, but that He loved us and sent His Son...for our sins." That's the good news!

Let me say it one more time...and I'll close with this. It happened at Christmas some time ago. The occasion was the annual presentation of Handel's "Messiah" at the Claremont Colleges in California. People were coming into the concert hall and being seated. A young man and a young woman of college age entered and sat down. The young man turned to the woman and said, "I don't know why I come to this thing every year. I don't believe any of it. It's all myth, just a big fairy tale."

The program began and proceeded through one magnificent number after another. The two students sat there and listened to the words of scripture expressed in that great musical setting:

> "Comfort ye, comfort ye my people—Behold a virgin shall conceive and bear a Son and shall call His name Emmanuel, God with us— The people who walked in darkness have seen a great light—For unto us a child is born—Behold I bring you good tidings of great joy which shall be to all people—For to you is born this day in the city of David, a Savior which is Christ the Lord—He shall feed His flock like a shepherd—Come unto Him, all ye that labor and are heavy laden, and He shall give you rest—Take His yoke upon you and learn of Him, for He is meek and lowly of heat, and ye shall find rest unto your souls."

The music stopped and the two students got up to leave. The young man again turned to the woman and said: "I really don't believe it, but every time I hear it, it sort of gets to me, you know?"

They thought they were through with God—all done with that Sunday School stuff. But God wasn't through with them. Through that lovely music He was reaching out to them. And it was Christmas again!

That's the good news—not that we love God, but that He loves us! It's a love that never quits, a love that never lets us go, a love that never stops loving. And the way we know about it is through the Word made flesh at Christmas.

That's why we sing, "Go, tell it on the mountain, over the hills and everywhere. Go tell it on the mountain that Jesus Christ is born!" We sing that joyfully because the message of Christmas is good news!

Prayer: Father, it's almost too good to be true, this good news of Your love made known to us in Jesus. Help us to believe it, to receive it in faith, to embody it in our lives, and to share it with the entire world. Thank you, Father, for Your inexpressible gift. Amen.

5.
What To Do With Yesterday

Psalms 103:8-12

One of the first things Patricia and I had to learn when we moved to Big Canoe was how to deal with our garbage. We learned very quickly that if we just let it sit there, it would begin to stink up our lives. It would invite all sorts of pests. It would make our lives unpleasant in a variety of ways. So, as a matter of regular discipline, we had to pack it up, load it in the car, and take it to the dump. We had to get rid of it.

Of course, there is more than one kind of garbage. The kind of garbage we put into our trash cans is relatively easy to discard. It just takes some planning, some effort. When we work at it, it is gone. But there is another kind of garbage that is more difficult to manage. It is the garbage of the past. A great many people have never learned how to deal with yesterday. Instead of looking to the future with hope, excitement, and positive expectation, they are bogged down in the past. They feel guilty about this. They are hurting over that. They are disappointed that they didn't do the other. They are bitter over the way they were treated. For so many people, the past is like a heavy weight around our necks, holding us back from the good future that God intends.

For so many of us, the negative parts of our past are like that piece of cellophane, clinging to us by static electricity. No matter what we do, it hangs on, irritatingly, distractingly. How can we focus on the future? How can we take hold of the promises of God to make all things new for us if we are so maddeningly focused on the past? We can't get on to new business because we are so bogged down in old business!

What is it in your past that keeps giving you a hard time? Is it something you did, and the guilt of it still hurts? Is it something you failed in and the disappointment of that will not let you go? Is it something someone else did to hurt you, and you keep rehearsing it, and the pain of it will not go away? Is it grief? Someone or something you once had and now have lost, and your life seems empty as a result?

Surely we understand that God does not intend for us to live like that. Our God is not a God of the past, but of the future. Our God is One who says again and again, "Behold, I am doing a new thing." "If any one is in Christ, there is a new creation. The old has passed away; behold everything is new!" Listen, I am sure of this: whatever is hurting you, whatever is holding you back, whatever is keeping you from the fullest possible experience of life, God wants to gather it up, and like some conscientious garbage collector, take it away so it will never bother you again. God will do that, if you will let Him.

Isn't that the message of our scripture? "As the heavens are high above the earth, so great is His steadfast love toward those who fear Him; as far as the east is from the west, so far does God remove our transgressions from us." Won't we understand once and for all: God is not in the condemnation business, God is in the redemption business. He looks at our past not to find ways to condemn us, but to discover what's holding us back, so that He can take it away and free us for life in the future. That's what God is interested in, not the past, but the future! He wants us to have a good future. So, He wants to take away from us all that gets in the way of that future. That's not a bad image, is it? God, as the great and loving garbage collector of the world.

Not too long ago I did some marriage counseling with a couple experiencing difficulty in their marriage. They had been through some troubling financial times, in debt and out of work. During that time the tension had been great, and they had said and done some very hurtful things to one another. Now, things are better financially. They are both working in good jobs. They have enough money to meet their needs. They sat in my office and told me that, looking only at their present reality, there is no good reason they should not be happy, and in love. But, the past, that stubborn, painful past. They can't let go of it. They keep on re-living it. They keep picking at the scabs until they are bleeding again, refusing to let healing take place. They keep bringing up those painful chapters of their past and beating one another over the head with it. Do you understand? If it weren't for their past, they could have a happy future!

I tried to give them a concrete visual image they could focus on. I asked them to visualize themselves as little tugboats, towing behind them a huge barge loaded down with garbage. The barge is connected to them by a steel cable and it follows them wherever they go. It slows them down. It saps their energy. It keeps them from going to some good places where, otherwise, they could go. And, it stinks up the place wherever they are! That's their past. It's a huge barge, loaded down with garbage, the garbage of guilt and regret and hurt.

Going further with the image, I told them that there are not many good things they can do with their garbage from the past. First, they cannot un-do it. You can't go back and change the past, relive the past. No, once it's happened, it's happened, and there is no point in pretending that it hasn't. The sins and failures and disappointments and hurts of the past are real. That's the truth of it. Second, it's not wise simply to repress our garbage. It does us no good to shove the past down into our unconscious and pretend that it's not there. No, repression does not last. Sooner or later, in some way or other, it's going to surface and give us some trouble. Third, I told them that they can't blame it on someone else. If we sift though all the garbage of our lives, we will discover that we are the common denominator. We might as well claim ownership of it. It's our garbage!

Do you hear what I told them? There is not much good we can do with the garbage of the past: we can't undo it, we can't repress it, we can't disown it. There are only two good things we can do with the past: we can allow God to forgive it, and we can allow God to help us learn from it. We can allow God to cut the cable on our barge and allow it to float away forever. And we can allow God to help us learn painful lessons from the past, so that we don't accumulate quite as much garbage in the future. Remember, God is far more interested in the future than in the past. God has promised to cut us free from the past so that we can move unhindered into a good future. That's what our scripture promises: "As far as the east is from the west, so far does God remove our transgressions from us."

As we begin this new year, we want to begin it with hope, with enthusiasm, with the assurance that God will accompany us into the future and that He will make it good. We want to move into the new year uncluttered with all the garbage of the past. I want to suggest several steps in that process.

First, we take yesterday's garbage, we name it and we claim it. We tell it like it is and we acknowledge that it has our name on it. It's our garbage! Naming it is what we mean by confession. We take whatever is cluttering up our lives and diluting the divine image in us—we take that and call it by name. We are too inclined to pray, "God forgive me for my sins." In my mind, I hear God say, "Such as..." The more specific we can be in our confession, the more specific can be our forgiveness. There is profound truth in the Biblical idea that if you know the name of the demon giving you trouble, you can gain power over it. So, to know the name and to speak the name of your demon in confession enables God to give you power over it. That's the first step. We name it and we claim it.

Second, we learn from it. We allow God to bring something good out of it. One of the great truths of our faith is that in God's economy, nothing need be lost. We can learn from our mistakes. We can be strengthened by our disappointments. We can become more loving and sensitive to others as a result of our hurts. We can draw closer to God through the experience of sins forgiven. So, if we know how to look for it, and how to nurture it, by the grace of God we can find flowers growing up even in the midst of our garbage dump. Do you understand that part of the good news? Absolutely nothing can happen to us that God cannot use for good, if we will let Him. Our God is able to make a resurrection out of every crucifixion, an Easter out of every Good Friday. And, in hands strong enough to do that, you and I are always safe and secure!

One final thing: we name our garbage and claim it as our own. We learn from it and we allow God to bring good from it. And then, finally, we allow God to cut the cable and to take our garbage away.

I don't know where some people get their pictures of God—certainly not from Jesus. I don't understand Christians who see God as One just looking for some excuse to punish us, to exclude us from His love, One who keeps pouring over the past and dredging up old sins, old failures, old hurts and beating us over the head with them. That's not God. God is not the accuser—Satan is. God doesn't want to hold our past over our head like some threatening guillotine. No, God wants to set us free from all that hurts us, discourages us, and makes us to think less of ourselves. Because God loves us, He wants only good for us. Won't you hear that? The problem is not that God is reluctant to forgive us. The problem is that we are reluctant to forgive ourselves. The problem is that it seems too good to be true that there is no sin that God is not anxious to forgive. God wants to forgive us even more than we want to be forgiven. Because what God wants for us is to live today and tomorrow and all the tomorrows of our lives as His beloved sons and daughters, secure in the warmth of His love, and walking in the wonderful light of His Way.

Listen to the promise of scripture: "If we confess our sins, He is faithful and just and will forgive us our sins, and cleanse us from all unrighteousness." "As far as the east is from the west, so far does God remove our transgressions from us." And those words from the cross: "Father, forgive them, for they do not know what they are doing." Do you hear the good news? God is not in the condemnation business. God is in the redemption business.

While I am talking about forgiveness, I must take a moment to say that not only do we need to be forgiven by God. We need, also, to forgive those who have sinned against us. And not just for their sake, even more for our sake. That's garbage too, you know: the hurt, the resentment, and the anger toward others. As long as we are carrying that around with us, it is difficult to move into a new and better future. I remember talking with a woman whose husband left her and married another. When talking about forgiveness, she said, "I'm not ready to forgive him yet. He hasn't suffered enough." But, he had remarried and gotten on with his life. He was not suffering because of her lack of forgiveness. She was. Every day she was being consumed by her bitterness and anger. And, her children and everyone around her were affected by the stink of it. When God cuts the cable, he takes that kind of garbage away, too.

Listen to the good news: there is no sin God is not willing to forgive. There is nothing you can do to make God stop loving you. There is nothing you can do to make God love you more than He already does. Right now, you are the loved, forgiven, blessed children of God. And the future can be good for you, if you will let God cut that cable!

I want to tell you about someone who learned that lesson. Arthur Gordon was one of the brightest students ever to graduate from high school in Savannah, Georgia. He received a full scholarship to Yale University. Then, he became a Rhodes Scholar and studied at Oxford University in England. After the Second World War, he and some of the people he had met in school decided to publish a literary journal, with him as editor. But, however brilliant a scholar, he was no business man. The enterprise went broke and he filed for bankruptcy. In the meanwhile, his high school sweetheart became tired of waiting for him to get his feet on the ground, so she married someone else. This man, who had been a success at everything he had tried in his life, suddenly experienced failure for the first time. He was a dismal failure, and he fell quickly and deeply into depression.

His family was concerned about him and persuaded him to go to a counselor in New York City. He was desperately in need, so he went, and he unpacked his heart. He told the counselor everything, everything that had happened, everything he felt. He confessed his sins. He talked of his despair and hopelessness about the future. He held nothing back. He told it all.

When he had finished his story, the counselor said that he wanted Arthur to listen to some tape recordings of sessions he had had with other clients, all anonymous, of course. So, he listened as a father confessed the ways he had failed his wife and children. He listened as a wife confessed her faults in a failed marriage. He listened as a research scientist confessed to mistakes in the laboratory. When the tape recorder had been turned off, the counselor asked, "Do you hear any similar themes being sounded in all these tapes?" "Yes," Arthur said, "they all keep saying, 'If only I had done differently.'"

"Exactly", said the counselor. "I was able to help every one of them. They are all very different people now. And, the way I helped them was this: Instead of saying, 'If only,' I taught them to say, 'Now, next time...'"

Do you hear what he was saying? You can't change the past, so it doesn't do any good to keep saying, "If only..." But the future, the future is still fluid, still able to be shaped, still open with all kinds of possibility. When we begin to say, "Next time..." we are saying that we have learned from the past, but it is just that, the past. Our future is not in bondage to it.

His sessions with the counselor changed Arthur Gordon's life. He changed his way of thinking about the past and the future. Instead of saying, "If only..." he began to say, "Next time..." He said that what he learned there was far more important than anything he had learned at Yale or at Oxford.

He might not have said it like this, but what he learned was the gospel. There is not much good you can do with yesterday's garbage. You can hang on to it. But if you do, it will stink up your life and deny you any good future. So, it's far better to handle it God's way. And God's way is this: you confess it, learn from it, and then allow God to cut the cable and take it away. That's the promise.

With the full authority of God, I say to you, "In the name of Jesus Christ, we are forgiven. As far as the east is from the west, so far does God remove our transgressions from us." The future is open, and the future, God's future, will be good! Thanks be to God!

Prayer: Loving God, our Father, help us to trust You enough to trust You with our past and with our future. Forgive us and cut us free from the past. Help us to learn needed lessons from it. And, above all, assure us that you accompany us into a grace filled future, a future that You will make good for all of us. In the Master's name we pray. Amen.

6.
Wrestling for a Blessing

Genesis 32:22-30

The all night wrestling match with God reveals much of the meaning of Jacob's life. The verses I just read report the events of only a few hours, but in those hours we see the meaning of his whole life.

Jacob's entire life had been a struggle. From the very beginning, he struggled with his twin brother, Esau. Jacob was his mother's favorite. But he knew that Esau, his brother, was his father Isaac's favorite. It was a classic sibling rivalry which resulted in tragic consequences. You remember the story: with the encouragement of his mother, Jacob conspired to steal Esau's birthright and blessing. In fear of his life, he ran away from home. He went to a far away land and fell in love. He agreed to work for seven years in return for Rachel's hand in marriage. But, his future father-in-law, Laban, was fully as much of a scoundrel as was Jacob. On the wedding night, Laban substituted his older daughter, Leah for Rachel. So, Jacob had to work for seven more years for Rachel, whom he really loved. Love was getting expensive! Then Jacob and Laban got into a dispute over possessions. First Laban cheated Jacob, and then Jacob cheated Laban. Their family reunions must have been something! The point is, life was a constant struggle for Jacob. Most of it he brought on himself, but it was a struggle!

From the very beginning Jacob was a man of deceit and cunning. Even in the womb, the story says, he grabbed Esau's heel, trying to keep him from being born first. His name, Jacob, means "supplanter." One commentator nicknamed him "grabber"—he grabbed his brother's heel; he grabbed his brother's birthright; he grabbed some property from Laban. Early in his life, he was not a very nice person, this Jacob. Not the sort of person you would want for a neighbor, and not for a brother either, for that matter.

But something happened to him that night in the wilderness. He had an all night wrestling match with God and came away from that encounter a new man. In the midst of the wrestling, Jacob said, "I will not let you go unless you bless me." So, God blessed him. And his name was changed from Jacob to "Israel," meaning "one who strives with God." Jacob's sons were the founders of the tribes of Israel. Since his time, all the people of Israel have traced their ancestry back to him. They say, proudly, "We are the descendents of Abraham, Isaac, and Jacob."

I see in this story a basic truth about life. Listen now, because I'm about to say something important: Jacob's newness came to him as a result of struggle. What I have discovered and what you will discover, if you have not discovered it already, is that most significant growth, most progress, comes to us also, as a result of struggle. I'm not altogether sure why that is so, but I know that it is. I'd like to say some things about that now in today's sermon.

Thank God, many of the blessings of life do not require struggle—the gift of life itself, this wonderful world with all its beauty and abundance, the love of family and friends and God—all are gifts of sheer grace, simply given to us. But growth is something else. Physical growth, intellectual growth, emotional growth, spiritual growth—almost all of that does not come easily. There is struggle involved.

Everyone I know is in favor of growth. We don't want to stagnate. We do want to grow in all the ways that growth is possible. At the same time, there is something in every one of us that resists growth. Growth means change. Change means risk. And risk is scary. There is something about us that, although we are in favor of growth, at the same time we like the familiar, the safe, and the tried and true. I can identify with the Australian bushman who said that he liked his new boomerang well enough, but he had a hard time throwing the old one away! That's us. We have difficulty discarding the old. We like to cuddle up with the familiar and the comfortable.

In fact, throughout life, the lure of the comfortable and familiar is so strong that probably we are not going to move away from them unless something happens to blast us out of our complacency. Probably some new life experience must come to us—some experience which calls into question our previous way of thinking, or feeling, or acting, or relating. Apart from that, we'll probably just keep on thinking and doing the same ol', same ol' stuff.

Sometimes the struggle that makes for growth is simply a tension between an old idea and a new one. For years all sane and stable people knew that human beings could never fly. But when the Wright brothers flew their airplane, the world had to adjust its thinking—but not without a struggle. Centuries ago, some crazy people came along insisting that the world is round instead of flat. They were ridiculed and persecuted until someone sailed around the globe and reached the east by sailing west. We've had to change our way of thinking—but not without a struggle. In fact, some people haven't given up yet. In England there is a group of people called "The Flat Earth Society," still stubbornly insisting that the earth is flat!

An old, false, or inaccurate idea will not be released until it is pushed out of our minds by a new and better idea. I may insist that the sum of two and two is three—I may invest myself emotionally in that contention—and I will stubbornly hold on to that until someone, in the battle of ideas, proves to my satisfaction that the correct sum is four. Without such a conflict of ideas there is no intellectual growth. Such growth is often difficult and painful. It does not come without the struggle of ideas.

Now, as difficult and painful as that is, even more difficult is the growth occasioned by changes in our life situation. We lose a job, or we take on a new job. We experience divorce or difficulty in our family. We experience a terrorist attack or a natural disaster. A financial reversal comes to us. We or a loved one becomes ill. Someone close to us dies. Someone we care about betrays us or disappoints us. We are presented with an opportunity and our resources are inadequate. You could add to this list, but you know what I am talking about: something happens to shake us to our foundation. All of our trusted ways of coping are called into question and we are forced to grow. We have to think new thoughts, or try new things, or reach out for new resources. That's all called growth!

It's frightening. It's unsettling. Often it's painful. But without such experiences we would not grow. I'm convinced of it. We would settle down and become comfortable with far less than our best efforts. The familiar and the safe would become good enough for us, and we would never become all that we can be.

Sometimes a person will start growing, find it scary and painful, so they turn and run away. They retreat into the familiar and the comfortable. And they begin to die. As much as I regret that, I do understand it, because to grow is to move out into uncharted territory. It is much like the struggle of the butterfly to extricate itself from the cocoon. It's a bit scary, I am sure, because the butterfly doesn't know what it is like "out there." It does know what the cocoon is like. How tempting to return to the safe, familiar, warm surroundings! But, of course, to do so would be to die, and to miss out on the experience of dancing through the air as a butterfly!

I believe that growth always takes us in a good direction, but often that good direction requires even more struggle. I have discovered that not everyone applauds our growth. I remember seeing a cartoon depicting a prince and a princess talking. The princess says to the prince: "I liked you better as a frog!"

A classic pattern of marriage has two neurotic people adjusting to one another and functioning fairly well in a sick sort of way. Then one partner begins to grow in the direction of health and the relationship begins to be in trouble. The two don't fit as well any more. Sometimes that prompts the other partner to get well too. But, sometimes it leads to the break-up of the marriage. Don't imagine that growth is always sweetness and light. It can be extremely painful.

I can't tell you how many members of congregations I have served have said to me, "Jim, I wish there were some way to grow without experiencing so much pain." I do too, but I don't know of any. Just as the blessing came to Jacob as a result of his wrestling, so growth comes to us as a result of our struggle. At least it can, if we do it in the right way.

Bobby Jones, one of the greatest golfers in the history of the game once said, "I never learned anything from the matches I won. All I know about golf I learned from the matches I lost." I understand. As I look back over my life, it is absolutely clear to me that the greatest times of personal growth have been the times of greatest pain and struggle.

In my first pastorate after graduating from seminary, all starry-eyed and idealistic, I ran headlong into a social revolution that threatened to chew me up and spit me out. Everything I believed in was called into question. All my relationships were tested. My foundations were shaken. My whole life and character as a Christian was at stake. Confusing? Frightening? Painful? You bet it was. But it was also a time of remarkable growth. Never have I felt closer to God. And I learned some things about myself and about the Christian gospel that I will never forget.

Then I was assigned the task of organizing a new congregation. I've never encountered a more difficult task. I worked long hours. Members of the family were sick. We went deeply into debt. I came very close to an emotional breakdown. But, in retrospect, it was a time of significant growth, in large measure because of the struggle.

There was a time when, at the invitation of a friend, I attended a seminar. Some very polished and persuasive people were presenting some new ways of thinking about God and about the Christian faith. It was a direct challenge to so much of what I believed. I tell you, my world was shaken! I didn't sleep for a number of nights. I wasn't sure what I believed or why. But that painful experience sent me back to my study to read and sort out. It sent me to my knees in prayer. And that experience helped me to build a solid foundation of faith which I believe can stand up to anything. But, don't you see, without the challenge I would not have put forth the effort. Without the pain, I would not have opened myself so completely to God. It's true: without the struggle, there is not the growth.

Everything I have said about individual growth is also true about growth in relationship. Patricia and I celebrated another wedding anniversary last May, and I wouldn't go back to the honeymoon for anything. It's better now. But what many people don't understand is that it's better not in spite of the difficulties we have experienced together, but in large measure because of them. I have come to believe that the only way you can have depth in any relationship is to share some struggles together.

Do you remember the beautiful story of Helen Keller and her teacher, Anne Sullivan? Helen was born blind and deaf. It was an almost insurmountable challenge to establish communication with her, teach her, and help her to develop the distinctive gifts which were hers. A lesser person than Anne Sullivan could not have done it. It was a struggle from the very beginning. The two of them literally wrestled with each other from time to time as the tedium and the frustration grew. It was the story of Jacob all over again. Finally they established a method of communication of tapping out letters of words on the lips. And, the first words Helen Keller tapped out on Anne's lips were, "I love you." Not only did their wrestling with one another produce two remarkable human beings, their shared struggle also led to a lifelong, close, caring relationship. That's the way it works!

Of course, struggle does not automatically and inevitably lead to growth. It does not always take us in good directions. We all know people who have allowed difficulty to make them bitter and resentful. Instead of growing, they regressed. How sad. We don't have any choice about whether or not our lives will be touched with difficulty. They will be. You can count on it. Our choice is about what we will do with the difficulty once it comes. Victor Frankl called it the last human freedom. It is the freedom to decide what our attitude will be in any given circumstance. Okay, here is the difficulty. Here is the struggle. What are you going to do with it?

There is a poem that says it:

> "One ship sails east, another west
> By the self same winds that blow.
> It's the set of the sail and not the gale
> That determines the way they go."

So, what are you going to do with it, this difficulty that comes to us all? When Jacob was in his wilderness, he encountered God. And the two of them went at it. And out of it, Jacob received a blessing. One reason struggles often lead to blessings, is that in struggle we recognize our limitations and our weaknesses, so, we reach out for resources beyond ourselves. It's just as Paul said, "When I am weak, I am strong." Do you understand? When we think we are strong, we have only our own strength, our own resources, and in the face of life's difficulties, that is really weakness. But, when we realize our limitations, we open ourselves to God and all the resources of faith, and then we can become strong.

We have all been through a lot in recent years. Today is the fourth anniversary of September 11, 2001. Our nation is at war in Iraq. We have been shaken by the disaster that is Hurricane Katrina. And every one of us has experienced difficulties in our personal lives and in the lives of loved ones. How do we set our sail when the difficulties of life attack us? On what foundation do we stand? How do we cope?

Here is what I believe. Here is the foundation on which I stand. I believe that God is. I believe that God is like Jesus. His name is love. And in every moment of every day He is at work for our good. His powerful hands took a crucifixion and turned it into a resurrection. And He can do it again and again. No matter what problems we encounter, no matter what struggles we face, there is absolutely nothing that God and us together can't handle. If we are open to it, out of every difficulty God can bring growth. Out of every struggle God can produce a blessing!

That most loved hymn says it:

"Through many dangers, toils and snares I have already come;
'Tis grace hath brought me safe thus far, and grace will lead me home."

Do you hear it? By the grace of God, every struggle can be used for blessing. I believe that. I trust that! Because I have experienced that!

Prayer: Father, we don't like the struggle. But we trust that there is nothing in life that You cannot use for good. So, in every difficulty, help us to turn to You. Take our weakness and make it strength. Take our struggles and turn them into blessings, as You did with Jacob, and Jesus, and Jim. In Jesus' name we pray. Amen.

7.
Conviction With Compassion

John 8:3-11

You and I are living today in the midst of a massive moral muddle. There is pervasive confusion or indifference concerning what is right and wrong. And, some people are wondering whether or not such terms should even be used. After all, we are being told again and again that all values are relative, that standards of behavior change from generation to generation. We have seen it happen that an action which is declared unacceptable in one decade is approved in the next.

So, people throughout our land are beginning to believe that there is no fixed point on the moral compass. The watch-words of our generation are "freedom," and "broad-mindedness." Our mottos are: "Do your own thing!" "Grab all the gusto you can, you only go around once!" "Live for the moment!" "If it feels good, do it!"

Increasingly, that's the spirit of our time. Whereas the people of former generations were fearful of the consequences of immoral behavior, that is not the fear of most of our contemporaries. A great many of our contemporaries are most fearful of being labeled "narrow-minded" or "old fashioned." Almost above all things, a great many people want to be liberated, up to date, "with it."

I wish I could celebrate such attitudes. There is a part of me that would like to join the mass migration into a more permissive future. I don't enjoy being out of step with so many others, and I certainly don't like to be called "old fashioned." But, at some points, I am; I have to be, because, as a pastor, I see where our moral confusion is taking us. Every week I am called upon to help straighten out the wreckage of someone's life. And all too often the hurt has been inflicted because someone began to believe that what history has taught us about right and wrong is somehow no longer applicable. They discover too late that, contrary to popular wisdom, God's moral laws have not been repealed, and that what we sow, we reap.

I'm talking about the full sweep of the moral landscape: scandals in government; kickbacks in business; the rape of the environment; a nation so undisciplined that we refuse to live within our income; the aids epidemic; abortions numbering in the millions; pre-marital and extra-marital sexual activity; half of marriages ending in divorce; physical, sexual, emotional abuse within the family; drug and alcohol abuse; crime so rampant that millions of people live in constant fear; the stubborn scourge of racism; the growing curse of terrorism; pervasive lying, calling the light darkness and the darkness light; the placing of pleasure and possessions at the top of our list of values; an affluent culture tolerating hunger, homelessness, illiteracy and sub-standard health care; the world increasingly divided into the haves and the have nots; where would the list stop? I could go on and on, but you get the point. When you take a panoramic view of contemporary morality, are you content with what you see?

It is such a serious problem that I need to address it, using the scripture in the gospel of John as our point of reference. The questions are: how can we be moral without being moralistic? How do we make moral judgments without being judgmental? How do we let people know that we love them no matter what their behavior, without giving approval to behavior which is unacceptable? Let's look at the way Jesus did it.

I.

The first thing we see as we look at Jesus' encounter with the woman accused of adultery is that he made a moral judgment. She had sinned. Her behavior (and that of the man not mentioned in the story) was unacceptable, so Jesus condemned the behavior. Jesus' love for her did not require that he pretend her sin did not exist; in fact, just the opposite. It was precisely because he did love her that he had to identify and condemn the behavior that was hurting her.

We could use more of that kind of tough love. I wish we could learn once and for all that genuine love is not weak. It is not wishy-washy. Authentic love is strong. There are times when we must say, in love, "You are wrong. You made a mistake. You inflicted a hurt."

I believe that because we love, we have to make moral judgments. We must bring ourselves to say, "This is good. This is evil." I choose to believe that, morally speaking, everything is not up for grabs. I believe that there is behavior which God applauds and behavior which God deplores. I believe that there are paths that lead to life and others that lead to hurt and heartbreak. And what makes right right and wrong wrong is not what the majority of people say, but what God says! That is the way it is because this is God's world and God is in charge here!

I don't believe there is anything unique about our generation which cancels out what history has shown us to be good and true and life-giving. I have seen too many people discover all too late, amid their tears, that morality is not a matter of indifference. There is a way that leads to life and there is a way that leads to destruction. And the way that leads to destruction needs to be identified and labeled. We must make moral judgments!

It is not good news for someone to say that there is no such thing as good and evil, therefore it doesn't make any difference what I do. Don't you see, if my behavior is a matter of indifference, then my life is a matter of indifference. I can choose anything, live any old way, and it doesn't matter. That is not good news. That is bad news. It is saying that my life doesn't count. You life doesn't count. And that is what we human beings fear more than anything else—that, finally, our lives don't count.

The good news is that this is God's world. God created us to live in relationship with Him, in a loving, trusting, obedient relationship. He calls us to the highest possible standards of behavior, and He cares about what we do. There is a great deal at stake in the decisions we make. Don't you see how ennobling that is? Our lives count for something, because God Himself cares what we do!

I don't know about you, but I don't want to be so broad-minded that I don't stand for anything. I don't want my moral vision to become so blurred that I begin to call the darkness, light, and the light, darkness.

Look at the story from John's gospel. Jesus' love for the adulterous woman did not prevent him from calling her actions sinful. Indeed, his love for her required that he do precisely that. Anything less would have indicated that she didn't count, that what she did with her life didn't matter. Don't you see, such broad-mindedness is not love. Such acceptance of unacceptable behavior is not love. It is the very antithesis of love. Because Jesus loved her, he said, "You have sinned." That's the first thing I want to say: we must make moral judgments. Love demands it.

II.

It is true, as I have said, that we must make moral judgments. Otherwise, life has no meaning. But, we must make moral judgments without being judgmental. That is the second thing we must see in the text from the gospel of John. And that is why Jesus had some words for those self-righteous people with stones in their hands, preparing to pound the life from her body as a penalty for her sin.

Please hear what I say now with your ears and minds wide open, because it is essential to the issue at hand. As Christians, we are to make moral distinctions, but never from the position of self-righteousness. That is what Jesus was getting at when he said, "Don't judge." He was not telling us not to make moral judgments. We must do that. He was telling us to avoid self righteousness. We may identify someone's behavior as unacceptable or as sinful, but we must never assume that we are, therefore, better than they. The sinful behavior we see in another person may not be our particular problem, but we have sins of our own which will do just fine to keep us from any sense of moral superiority.

The fact is, "all have sinned and have fallen short of the glory of God." The word is "all", and I presume that includes you as it includes me. Jesus never glossed over the sinful woman's behavior. He never excused it. He never approved of it. But, he did say to the mob that they were not to punish her unless they could claim sinless perfection.

Of course, no human being can claim such perfection. Each of us is in need of the love and forgiveness of God. Our relative moral superiority or inferiority begins to pale into insignificance when seen in the light of our common need for God's mercy. So, we are never to feel better than, or superior to, any other human being. It is clear from the gospel that a person's worth is not derived from behavior, but from our common status as the children of God. Therefore, we are all of equal worth in the eyes of God because we are all His children. We always go wrong when we attach worth to behavior. We always go wrong when we use behavior as a way of dividing the world into the good people and the bad people, the worthy people and the unworthy people, usually placing ourselves among the good and the worthy. We must make moral judgments, but we must never become proud and judgmental.

Admittedly, that is a difficult balance to maintain. How easy it is to become unloving and ungracious in the name of moral standards. I am thinking at this moment about an accountant who has impeccable moral standards. His ethical behavior is above reproach. But he uses ethical standards like a club with which to punish people. He is so unloving, so unforgiving, so ungracious in his morality. I like the prayer of a little girl: "O God, make the bad people good, and make the good people nice!" A great many good people could be so much nicer! What we are looking for is morality without stuffiness, goodness without arrogance.

Look at the contrast between the mob and Jesus on that day. Jesus was uncompromising in his standards. But he applied those standards lovingly, because what he wanted was not punishment, but new life.

The mob also had high standards, at least as far as sexual morality was concerned, but they applied their standards self-righteously and brutally in an effort to destroy life. We are to have convictions, yes! Strong convictions! But those convictions are to be applied always with compassion, with the intent to bring redemption and new life to every situation.

III.

One final thing: we are to have moral convictions—convictions of the highest order. We are to apply those standards to ourselves and to those around us. The place to start, of course, is with ourselves. We must never expect of others a higher standard of morality than we expect of ourselves. We Christians are to shape our culture and not to be shaped by it. There must be something distinctive about us. We must not blend comfortably and easily into the confusion of the prevailing moral backdrop. We must allow the Christ who lives within us to reshape us in his likeness. Then, by his grace, we are to live above the prevailing standards around us. We are to act as leaven in the loaf, salt in the food, light in the darkness. And, as we live above the prevailing cultural standards, we help to raise those standards.

But, and this is the key point, and the third thing I want to say: if our high standards are violated by others, if sins are committed, we are never justified in cutting the offenders off from our love and concern. The proper Christian response is not condemnation, but forgiveness; not a sneer, but a tear! Everyone must be welcome in the community of faith. No one must be excluded. What looks and sounds like Jesus? Jesus never excluded anyone. And, after all, the community of faith is where you get new life. Where else would you want sinners to be except here, among people of faith, among those made new by the saving, forgiving love of Christ?

That is the moral tightrope we Christians are called to walk. We are to make no compromise with the highest moral standards. We are to ask for and expect high levels of ethical behavior from ourselves and from others. We are to ask for that and expect that precisely because we are loving people and because we care about what happens to people. And surely we understand by now that God makes moral demands upon us not to inhibit us, but to give us the fullest possible experience of life. That is why He asks so much of us. So, I repeat, we must not make any compromise with the highest standards.

At the same time, we must never make our love conditional upon a person's behavior. As I have said, a person's worth has nothing to do with his or her behavior. Even when a person sins, he is still a child of God, so we are to reach out in love and extend the offer of forgiveness.

The fact is, it is when we deserve such love the least that we need it the most. And, that is exactly why grace is such good news!

The fact is, how we respond to sinful people will reveal clearly the extent to which we have received God's gifts. If we have been loved, then we will love. If we have been forgiven, then we will forgive. As followers of Jesus, we must never be found saying, "I will love you when...," "I will love you if...," "I will love you as long as..." No, our love must be unconditional. Our response is to say and mean, "I love you, period. I forgive you, period."

Looking again at our scripture, we see that Jesus had no interest in punishing the adulterous woman. Can't we understand once and for all that Jesus is not in the punishment business? Jesus is in the redemption business. The mob was calling for punishment, but not Jesus. Jesus was interested in helping the woman find new life. He did that, not by pretending that she had not sinned, not by saying that her behavior did not matter—indeed, he told her to change her ways, not to continue her sinful behavior. But, he let her know that his love for her was not contingent upon that. The change he asked for was not for him, it was for her, because in that direction was abundant life!

The story is one of the most beautiful in the Bible. Jesus confronted the angry mob, ready at any moment to begin pounding the flesh from her body. He said, "He who is without sin among you, let him cast the first stone." One by one they dropped their stones and quietly walked away. Then Jesus turned to the woman, huddled there on the ground, shivering in fear, and said, "Where are your accusers? Has no one condemned you?" She looked around and saw that everyone had gone. She replied, "No one, Lord!" Jesus said, "Neither do I condemn you. Go, and do not sin again." Isn't that beautiful? There is no doubt about it: Jesus has some convictions about behavior, about right and wrong. But he always applies those convictions with compassion, with love and forgiveness.

Let me paint a picture of it. A number of years ago, at her annual birthday honors party, Queen Elizabeth honored John Profumo. Do you remember him? John Profumo was a high ranking cabinet official in the British government, and was the major figure in a scandal that rocked the British Empire. A book, and later a movie, was made about the incident. The press reported that Profumo was involved in an affair with a call girl in London who, in turn, was involved with Russian spies. This was at the height of the Cold War. When this matter was brought to light, Profumo made the matter worse by lying to the House of Commons. Later, he had a change of heart, went to the Prime Minister, confessed, and resigned from the Cabinet in shame. He dropped from public notice and quietly went to work in the slums of London, attempting to be of help to the lonely and the lost. For him, I suppose, it was a kind of personal penance. Years passed. Then, when he was sixty years old, at the honors party, Elizabeth, the Queen of England, named John Profumo, the sinner, among the distinguished citizens of her realm! Isn't that great? He was restored. Restored! Now note, the Queen did not say that what he did is okay. What she said is that what he did is forgiven!

That is our stance. That is our Christian stance. We are to have the highest possible standards, asking, "What looks and sounds like Jesus?" But, we don't use our standards as a club with which to punish people, but as a call to fullness of life in Christ. And, when a brother or a sister stumbles, we don't accuse and condemn, we forgive and extend a helping hand. As followers of Jesus, we are to be people of conviction, but also, we are to be people with compassion.

Prayer: God, our Father, save us from moral indifference, from ethical wishy-washiness, from behavioral blindness. Help us to insist upon the highest standards from ourselves and from others, precisely because we care about them. Give us the spirit of our Lord. Help us to condemn the sin while accepting the sinner. Help us to love because we have been loved. Enable us to forgive because we have been forgiven. In Jesus' name we pray. Amen.

8.
The Church on Main Street

Matthew 28:16-20

During my years of ministry, church buildings have been located in a variety of places. There was Monterey Road, Clinton Boulevard, Culver Avenue, Gibbs Street, Duarte Road, Hardy Street. And in 1982, for the first time I became pastor of a church on Main Street. I've always thought that is where the church should be—not off on some side street somewhere—but on Main Street.

Of course, you know, when I talk about Main Street, I am not talking primarily about geography. I am talking about ideas and ministries. I believe that the task entrusted to the Christian Church is the most important on the face of the earth. It is far too important to neglect or misdirect.

When we spend our time answering questions no one is asking, while neglecting the deepest concerns of the human spirit, we have gotten off into side street religion. When we use our time, energy, and resources doing things that really don't need to be done, solving little, inconsequential problems, while neglecting the open sores of a hurting world, we have gotten off into side street religion. When we jump on the bandwagon of popularity and exhaust ourselves doing what other groups in society are doing, while neglecting that which only the Christian Church can do, we have gotten off into side street religion. And we are in danger of becoming what one cynic described as "a little company of people on a side street, singing ditties about heaven."

I remember hearing that during the bloody revolution in Russia, when all hell was breaking loose there, the leaders of the Russian

Orthodox Church were engaged in a heated controversy about the proper colors of the paraments in their churches. Side street religion!

Hear me loud and clear: trivial pursuit is a game we dare not play in the Church. The stakes are too high. The need is too great. All around us people are searching for answers, for a sense of direction. They are looking for a foundation to build on, some center of meaning to hold to. And I earnestly believe that we in the Christian Church have been entrusted with the very reality for which they search. What they are looking for is the God who has been revealed in Jesus. And, if we are not providing a connection between people and God, then we are traveling under a false identity. We have moved off Main Street, and we have little of value to offer to them or to anyone.

A few years ago, there was an article in the newspaper stating that Lawrence Rockefeller had given $21 million to Princeton University for the creation of a "Center for Human Values." The President of the University, Harold Shapiro, in announcing the gift said, "I hope this center will create a presence on campus to promote a lively discussion of the things that really matter." I read that and I thought to myself, "That's what the Church is supposed to be." We're supposed to be a group of people who belong to God, and who, consequently, deal daily with the things that really matter! It's when we do that that we move onto Main Street.

What are the things that matter? What are those things that are worthy of the investment of our time, our ability, our resources, our very lives? Well, Jesus tells us in the scripture I read a few moments ago. It is recorded in the 28th chapter of Matthew. It's the last thing Jesus said to his disciples. We pay close attention to last words, because usually they are very important. Listen now, because I'm about to say something important: the primary task of the Christian Church, given to us by Jesus himself is this: "Go...and make disciples of all nations, baptizing them in the name of the Father, and of the Son, and of the Holy Spirit, and teaching them to obey everything I have commanded you."

That's the task: if we want to be on Main Street; our task is to make Christian disciples. I remember seeing a poster that said: "The main thing in life is to make the main thing the main thing." Well, that's our main thing: to make Christian disciples.

What does it mean to be a disciple? That's what I want to talk about in the next few minutes. It's what every Church on Main Street will make the main thing.

I.

First, to be a disciple means that we belong to the God made known in Jesus, and we always will. Christian commitment is not just a Sunday thing, a sometimes thing. The Church is not a building to which we go or an organization to which we belong. It is our identity. It is who we are. You ask me who I am and I will tell you, "I am Jim McCormick, and I am one of the people of God. I belong to Him!"

I have learned a few things in my years of life. One thing I have learned is that the whole world is designed to function in a God-centered way. Nothing works out very well until we understand that and cooperate with that. Life is designed to function according to a "right order of things," with the God we have come to know in Jesus at the center, and with everything else deriving its meaning and direction from that vital center. Augustine was right: "Thou hast made us for Thyself, O God, and our hearts are restless 'til they find their rest in Thee."

If I didn't believe that, I don't know what I would believe. If I did not find meaning in Christ, I don't know where I would look for meaning. If my life were not centered in Christ, I would probably be wandering around out there somewhere, looking and looking and looking, and never finding. Because I really believe that until we allow God to take his rightful place at the center of life, nothing makes much sense, and nothing works out very well. That's one place our focus must be if we as a Church are to do business on Main Street! We belong to God and we always will. That's the first thing.

II.

Second, to be a disciple means that, just as we belong to the God made known in Jesus, we also belong to the family of God. Saying "Yes" to Christ and being converted is not the completion of the Christian process; it's just the beginning of it. God loves us and accepts us just as we are, but He doesn't leave us as we are. Once we are born into the Christian life by conversion, we then have to grow up to Christian maturity. That's a lifetime process and it happens in community. It happens in the Church.

So many people have mistakenly individualized the life of faith, as if it is only about getting cozy with God. But Biblical faith always involves a community of faith. In the Old Testament, faithful people were incorporated into the covenant community of Israel. In the New Testament, faithful people were incorporated into the covenant community of the church. Clearly, we belong to one another, because we all belong to the same God.

Because we belong to one another, we share life with one another. We weep with those who weep. We rejoice with those who rejoice. We call for and encourage the best within each other. And when we fall, our church family picks us up and helps to love the hurt away. No one of us is always strong and faithful. But when we are weak, we can ride piggy back on the faith of those who are strong. Then, when we are strong, they can lean on us. I have come to believe that we can face anything, we can deal with anything, as long as we don't have to face it alone, as long as there are those who love us and are willing to be with us. My church family is like a cheering section, saying, "Attaboy Jim, you can do it, you can make it, we're with you!" How can anyone make a go of life apart from that?

Wherever I am in the world, whatever I am experiencing, I am not alone. I am part of a family. And that makes all the difference. Years ago, they did an experiment at Marineland of the Pacific. They took a dolphin out of the community tank and placed him in isolation. Then they began to lower the temperature in the isolation tank, until the dolphin began to sink. He could not swim on his own. Then they took him out of the isolation tank and put him into the community tank. There, a remarkable thing happened: when he began to sink, one of the other dolphins began to swim underneath him, holding him up. Two other dolphins began swimming on each side of him, pressing their warm bodies against his, until his body temperature returned to normal and he was able to swim freely again! That is what the Church is supposed to be. We support one another when we are falling. We surround one another with warmth and love when we are hurting. Because I belong to Christ, I also belong to all those other brothers and sisters who also belong to Christ. The Church on Main Street will not let us forget that!

III.

Finally, to be a disciple means that we are on a mission in the name of Christ. We are to be on mission, 24 hours a day, seven days a week, for the rest of our lives.

If the God we have met in Christ is at the center, and we really belong to that God, then our constant prayer is, "Not my will, but Thine be done—Lord, what will You have me to do?" What would it look like to live your life like that? Not the usual prayer: "Not Thy will, but mine be done. Lord, help me to accomplish what is important to me." Not that, but really praying and meaning, "Lord, what will You have me to do? Today, with my life, right where I am?" I believe that if we pray that prayer and mean it, it will require at least these things:

First, we will find appropriate ways of telling the Christian story, the old story of Jesus and his love. Not only that, we will find ways to share what that story has done for us. When that is done simply and authentically, it is not arrogant or self righteous; it is just, as D.T. Niles put it, "One hungry person telling another hungry person where to get something to eat." We must tell the story by word and deed.

Second, we must claim that world out there for God and seek to shape it according to God's purposes. There are ways of living that lead to life and ways of living that lead to death. We are to shape the world in humane, compassionate, life-giving ways, in accordance with the intentions of the One who made it.

Finally, we must live servant lifestyles. Whatever the neighbor feels, we are to feel it. Whatever the neighbor needs, we are to supply it. Whatever the cost, we are to pay it, because we are to be servants of human need. The most profoundly disturbing ethical principle I know is found in the words of Jesus: "Just as you have done it to one of the least of these, my brothers and my sisters, you have done it to me." Does that mean what it says? That every hurting person in the world is Christ, and as we love and serve them, we are loving and serving Christ? That was the secret of Mother Teresa's ministry. She said, "In every person I meet, I see the face of Christ, and then I do something beautiful for God." Simply that. Simply and magnificently that! As followers of Jesus, we are to be servants of human need.

I'll never forget something that Harry Emerson Fosdick once said. He was pastor of Riverside Church in New York when their magnificent new building was built. But the last Sunday in their old building, before moving into the new one, he said: "My friends, it is not settled yet whether or not the new church will be wonderful. That depends upon what we do with it. If in that new temple we simply sit together in heavenly places that will not be wonderful. But if we also work together in unheavenly places, that will be." He was right on target. The validation of what we do in here, is what we then do out there as a result. When we are operating on Main Street, we understand that we Christian disciples are on mission in the name of Christ, and always will be!

Well, that's it. The task of the Church is to make disciples. And that means that we belong to God, we belong to one another as the family of God, and together we are on mission in the name of God. The center of it all is God. I don't know about you, but I don't want us to be a group of people on a side street singing ditties about heaven. I want us on Main Street, being about our Father's business, dealing with the things in life that really matter. And I am just as sure as I am sure about anything that the one to put us there and keep us there is Christ. And the good news is that we are not alone as we seek to be faithful disciples. Jesus gave us a big job, but he also gave us a big promise. He promised, "Remember, I am with you always, even to the end of the world." He is with us and his grace and strength are sufficient.

One closing image. Wes Seeliger is one of my favorite writers. Wes is a minister, but in some ways, a rather unconventional one. For one thing, he loves motorcycles. He tells about being in a motorcycle shop one day, drooling over a huge Honda 750 and wishing he could buy it. A salesman came up and began to talk about the bike. He talked about speed, acceleration, excitement, the attention-getting growl of the pipes when you revved it up, racing, risk! He talked about how all of the cute chicks are attracted to men who ride bikes! Then he discovered that Wes is a minister. Immediately he changed his language and even his tone of voice. He spoke quietly and talked about good mileage, high visibility. It was indeed a "practical" vehicle.

In writing about the experience later, Wes observed: "Lawn mower salesmen are not surprised to find clergymen looking at their merchandise. Motorcycle salesmen are. Why? Does this tell you something about the popular image of clergymen and of the Church? Lawn mowers are slow, safe, sane, practical, middle class. Motorcycles are fast, dangerous, wild, thrilling." Then Wes asked a question: "Is the Christian life more like mowing the lawn or like riding a motorcycle? Is the Christian life safe and sane, or dangerous and exciting? The common image of the Church is pure lawn mower: slow, deliberate, plodding. Our task is to take the Church out on the open road, give it the gas, and see what the old baby will do!"

I suspect that the best way to get to the Church on Main Street is by motorcycle!

Prayer: Father, forgive us for those times when we have become distracted and have lost our way. When we are at our best, we know that Your way is the way. So help us to keep You at the center of our lives and at the center of our life together, so that we may deal with the things that matter most in life, and so that, by Your grace, the things that matter most may be redeemed. Above all else in life, we do want to be faithful disciples. So, help us. In the name of Christ we pray. Amen.

9.
Vanilla, Chocolate, and Strawberry

I Corinthians 9:20-23, John 13:34-35

From the time Patricia and I first came to Big Canoe, almost four years ago, every day I have thought to myself, "What a rare privilege it is to live in this place, and especially to be a part of the faith community that is Big Canoe Chapel. So many people—so many rich histories—so many varied faith traditions! What a privilege to be here!" At the same time, every day I have thought to myself, "It is difficult to live graciously in the midst of so much diversity. We have to work at that every day!" Those two powerful feelings—side by side—every day!

Because we have come from many places, with many varied histories, and with many diverse faith traditions, each of us has customary ways of doing things. And, at least on the surface, it just feels better when things are done the way we prefer. That's the way we all are. The problem is, when there are so many sets of preferences, we can't do them all, all of the time. So, how can we feel comfortable and at home, when sometimes things are done in ways we don't like? I like to sing Sinatra's theme song, "I Did It My Way." But how do we sing that in a faith community when there is no one way that is everybody's way?

My father-in-law was in the ice cream business. Ervin Chunn was a great man, a sincere Christian, who was Vice-President of the largest ice cream manufacturing company in Mississippi. Whenever we were confronted with diversity, with a variety of opinions on any given subject, he would always smile and say, "That's why we make vanilla, chocolate, and strawberry." All those flavors are ice cream, but people have a variety of tastes. And, he was smart enough to know that if he made chocolate and only chocolate all the time, he would go out of business. So, he made them all. And, you know, I never found out what flavor was his personal preference. I'm a strawberry man myself. But I do think that those who prefer other flavors should have access to them, as long as I get some strawberry too.

Interestingly enough, the Apostle Paul had the same problem in the first century. Paul was passionate about the unity of the Christian community, our oneness in Christ. In one of his magnificent statements, he said, "There is neither Jew nor Greek, there is neither slave nor free, there is neither male nor female—you are all one in Christ Jesus." Talk about diversity! Talk about strong preferences! You had that in spades in the early Church!

They had Jewish Christians and Gentile Christians. They had free Christians and slave Christians. They had male Christians and female Christians. They had old Christians and young Christians. And all of that diversity brought problems with it. Just one case in point: the Jewish Christians had made a commitment to Christ as Savior and Lord, but they had been Jews all of their lives. And, they wanted to keep on doing their Jewish things: circumcision, Sabbath observance, dietary laws. And, because that's what they wanted to do, they thought that all Christians should do them. The Gentile Christians had never done those things, and they didn't see why they should have to start doing them now, just because they had come to faith in Christ. Those were matters of Jewish culture, not essential for salvation in Christ, so they didn't want to be bound by the Jewish law. Do you see the problem? Those diverse groups were supposed to worship together, eat together, live and love together, be in mission together, but they had different preferences, different lifestyles. Where could they find their unity?

Paul, almost single-handedly, stood astride the two groups and worked for unity and harmony in the Church. He was passionate about it. He agreed that the Gentile Christians should not be bound by the demands of the Jewish law—that was a matter of culture. And if the Jewish Christians wanted to continue doing them as a matter of culture, that was okay. Clearly, salvation was by faith in the God made known in Jesus, and not by circumcision, or Sabbath observance, or by diet. So, Gentile Christians should not be bound by those. But listen now: because unity was important, because their oneness in Christ was important, and because they were to worship together, eat together, live together, and be in mission together, they all needed to be sensitive to the things that were important to those who did not share their preferences. So, the Jewish Christians had to be careful not to impose their lifestyle preferences upon the Gentile Christians. And, at the same time, the Gentile Christians were to be sensitive to the Jewish Christians. When they sat down to eat together, the Gentiles should eat what the Jewish Christians ate, as a matter of sensitivity, as a contribution to their oneness. That's what love does.

Something like that is what Paul was getting at when he wrote his letter to the Church at Corinth. He was clear about what was central in the gospel, and he tried to make that clear to all the Christians. And, as to the matters which were not central to the gospel, he was intentionally flexible. He said, "To the Jews I became as a Jew—to the Gentiles I became as a Gentile—I have become all things to all people, that I might by all means save some."

Understand, he never compromised that which was at the heart of the gospel. But in all other matters, he was willing to do Jewish things if that made the Jewish Christians feel good. And, he was willing to do Gentile things if that made the Gentiles feel good. He wanted to provide something in that community of faith that made everyone feel accepted and welcomed. He practiced what I like to call, "holy hospitality"—something for everyone. That looks and sounds like Jesus to me.

You remember that Jesus was careful to welcome everyone, saint and sinner alike. He made time for and gave love to rich and poor, Jew and Gentile and Samaritan and Roman, rich and poor, sick and well, children and adults. He went to the Temple and worshipped there amidst the incense. At the same time, he preached and prayed along the dusty roads of Judea. Knowing that everyone is a child of God, he welcomed all. He loved all! And the religious leaders criticized him for it. They slung it at him with a sneer: "This man welcomes sinners—and eats with them!" But that's what makes the gospel the gospel!

Everyone who is successfully married knows the importance of what Jesus did, what Paul did, and what I am talking about. In marriage, if it is a good marriage, you can't do everything the way you prefer. You just can't. But when we are together in love, each partner sometimes willingly and even joyfully sacrifices his or her preference in order to give a gift of love to the partner. For example, I don't particularly enjoy shopping. It wears me out. But, I know that Patricia likes for me to go with her sometimes. So, I go. Not because that is my preference, but because it is a gift of love from me to her. At the same time, I enjoy sports. When watching television, Patricia much prefers a good movie. But sometimes she sits down and watches a golf match or a baseball game with me. Not because that is her preference—no, it is a gift of love from her to me. Not demands, but gifts, willing gifts because of love. So that, in marriage, two very different people will each have times in our comfort zone, encouraged to enjoy our preferences, not all the time, but some of the time. This strawberry lover will sometimes eat chocolate with Patricia, because I know she likes chocolate. And that chocolate lover will sometimes eat strawberry with me because she knows I like strawberry. That's what love does. And it looks and sounds like Jesus to me.

And that's why, at the Chapel, sometimes Lamar and I will wear clerical robes, and sometimes we will dress casually. Sometimes we will use language from the Book of Common Prayer, and sometimes we will be less formal. Sometimes we will sing classical music, and sometimes traditional hymns, and sometimes spirituals, and sometimes praise songs, sometimes accompanied by piano, sometimes accompanied by organ, sometimes accompanied by guitar. Sometimes some people clap, and others don't. Sometimes we will celebrate the Lord's Supper using wine and dipping into the chalice. Sometimes we will use grape juice and use individual cups. Sometimes we will pass the elements in the pews. We do a lot of different things at the Chapel, use different forms, different styles. Like Paul, we try to be all things to all people, knowing that no one is going to like everything we do. No one is going to be completely comfortable with everything we do. But, hopefully everyone will like some of what we do, and are willing to make gifts of love to others who have other preferences. For the sake of unity, for the sake of oneness, we will practice "holy hospitality," all of us, together, trying to provide a welcoming place for all of God's children.

I guess, because it is so difficult, and because it requires a high level of Christian maturity, few Christian groups even try it. One congregation serves vanilla. Another serves chocolate. Another serves strawberry. And, they say, "Choose your flavor." The Chapel is trying to serve some of it all, vanilla, chocolate, and strawberry, and more, because we know that some of God's people like them all. And we want to provide a place for all. And, that's difficult. It's difficult to find the right balance. That's why it's so rare. Kindergartners tend to say, "Mine!" And not want to share. It requires growth toward maturity to learn to share, and sometimes to set aside our preferences out of deference to others. But, when we pull it off, it is wonderful! When we pull it off, we allow our differences not to divide us, but to enrich us. I love the Chapel for that!

And, I don't know about you, but I need that. My life quickly becomes static and stale if I am always exposed only to what I already know and already like. Growth requires tension between where I am and where I am not, tension between what I am comfortable with and what I am not, tension between what I like and what I do not. Out of that creative tension comes learning! As one person wisely said, "One of my most important gifts to you is my difference from you." Of course! But I must be mature enough to recognize the truth of that, and then willingly listen to, learn from, work with, and love those whose preferences are different from mine. But when I do, when *we* do, it is wonderful. That is the church at its best: a welcoming atmosphere, an embracing spirit, holy hospitality. All of that looks and sounds like Jesus to me.

Please understand, I am not saying that, in the name of love, "anything goes!" Paul has helped us to make some important distinctions. In his second letter to the Corinthians, he said, "We have this treasure in earthen vessels, to show that the transcendent power belongs to God and not to us." Now, I know that what he meant by that is that the treasure of the gospel has been placed in the hands of very flawed people, like us. And that, in spite of our flawed condition, God has been able to do great things through the gospel. And that shows that the power of the gospel does not depend wholly upon our cleverness or goodness or hard work. The power of the gospel comes from God. That's what he was saying.

But let's take that image of the treasure and the earthen vessel and apply it to what we are talking about today. The treasure is the gospel, the good news of what God has done for us and for the world in and through Jesus. That is the treasure of the gospel and it is non-negotiable. It must not be changed, or compromised, or watered down. It's the treasure. But that treasure is always placed in cultural containers. The treasure of the gospel can be expressed in a great many forms and structures and styles. Our preference as to language, or dress, or music, or architecture, or liturgy, or style—those are not the gospel—those are containers through which the gospel is expressed. It is essential for us to know the difference. Too often religious people insist that their preference is the treasure. It is not.

It's okay to have preferences. We all do, and we all will. That's okay. What is not okay is, in the name of Jesus, to claim exclusive validity for our preferences. What is not okay is to say, in the name of Jesus, "As long as I get what I want, I don't care about what others want. I don't care whether this is a welcoming place, a place of holy hospitality." We can say that. We just can't say that in the name of Jesus! Now, I like strawberry. It's okay for me to like strawberry. It's even okay for me to believe and say that strawberry is the best. It's just not okay for me to say that only strawberry can be ice cream, and that those who prefer vanilla or chocolate are not real Christians—I mean, not real ice cream lovers.

I say all of this not to prepare you for some radical changes we intend to make. No, we will probably keep on doing much of what we have been doing. Most of our congregation is fairly traditional, so most of what we do will continue to be traditional. I say all of this to explain why we at least attempt to do a variety of things and embrace a variety of styles. You don't have to like everything we do. But can you feel good about trying to provide a welcoming atmosphere where others, with different tastes, can experience something of what they prefer?

I think I am growing in the spirit of Jesus. And the Chapel is helping me with that. There are still some things I prefer more than others. There are some things we do that make me less comfortable than others. I am not taste bud neutral. I do like strawberry. But I think I am at the place in life where I would not want to be a part of a congregation where everything was done exactly as I would like it done, because I would then think about all those other Christians who have other preferences. And by my insisting upon doing it my way, I would be separating myself from those with other preferences, and I would not be helping to create a welcoming atmosphere. I would be in my comfort zone, but not in a place of "holy hospitality." Will you help me struggle with all of that? Will you help me try to make the Chapel a place where everyone is welcome, and where we at least try to provide meaning-filled experiences for everyone?

I keep remembering that, shortly after my becoming Chaplain, some people left the Chapel. I remember one of them sitting in my office and saying, "I think the Chapel is too inclusive. I think you are too welcoming of too many different kinds of people." He thought it was a criticism. I think it was one of the greatest compliments we have ever received, because it is the same criticism made of Jesus.

And here is why: someone has suggested that all of life is a dress rehearsal for heaven. Have you ever thought about that? I suspect that there will be all kinds of people in heaven. There will be people with an infinite variety of preferences in heaven. I expect that we will have vanilla, chocolate and strawberry in heaven. And, if we can't get comfortable with that here, probably we won't be very happy there.

As I think about all of this, I can't help thinking about John Wesley. Wesley was an Anglican priest in England in the 18th century. He was not only Anglican, he was high church Anglican, very conservative liturgically. He thought the only place to worship was in a church, in a very formal setting, with a very traditional liturgy. You just don't worship or preach out of doors. You do that in a church! But, there were poor people, coal miners out in the countryside who couldn't get to church. They needed to hear the gospel too! So, traditional though he was, he went and preached in the out of doors. He hated it, but he did it. He wrote in his journal: "I consented to be more vile!" And, as he preached, those coal miners were so moved by the good news of God's grace, that their tears of joy made little rivulets in the coal dust on their cheeks.

Wesley had his preferences, but he did not allow those preferences to get in the way of the gospel. And he learned something: he learned that those worshiping in the churches with their formal liturgies and those worshiping in the out of doors near the mines were all one people, the people of God. And in spite of their differences they had one thing in common: they all were loved by God, and when they allowed that love into their hearts, they were able to love one another.

Wesley wrote in his journal: "Though we may not all think alike, may we not all love alike? May we not all be of one heart, even though we are not all of one opinion? Herein may all the children of God unite." That sounds like something Jesus said: "This is how everyone will know that you are my disciples, if you have love for one another."

That's what the Chapel is when we are at our best, and that's why I love being here. This is a place of holy hospitality, a place where we, willingly and joyfully, give one another gifts of love in order to make this a welcoming place. That looks and sounds like Jesus to me!

Prayer: Thank You, Father, for all Your gifts of love to us. Now help us, in the name of Jesus, to pass gifts of love on to others. In His name we pray. Amen.

10.
If We Had Known It Was You

Matthew 25:31-46

One of my favorite musical forms is the spiritual. For as long as I can remember, one of my favorite spirituals has been "Sweet Little Jesus Boy." I don't know why, exactly. I like the melody. I like some of the images it calls to mind. It stirs up some deep feelings within me. I don't know, I just like it.

But recently, some of the words have been troubling me. All throughout the song there is the recurring phrase, "We didn't know who you was," or, "We didn't know 'twas you." One typical verse says,

"The world treat you mean, Lord, treat me mean too;
But please, sir, forgive us Lord, we didn't know 'twas you."

Those words have been troubling me.

When our children were in their teen years, we took a long family trip. One of the highlights was a night when we went to Broadway in New York City and saw a production of "Godspell." In one of the scenes, Jesus gave his followers the message contained in our morning scripture. He said, "I was hungry and you gave me food. I was thirsty and you gave me drink. I was a stranger and you welcomed me. I was naked and you clothed me. I was in prison and you came to me." And then he added, "Just as you did it to one of the least of these, my brothers and my sisters, you did it to me." Jesus went on to talk about what would happen to those who did not feed the hungry, clothe the naked, visit the sick and imprisoned. And he concluded by saying, "Just as you did it not to one of the least of these, you did it not to me." At that moment, in the production of "Godspell," one of the female followers of Jesus began to slink off. And she, almost casually, tossed back over her shoulder the line, "If we had known it was you, Jesus, we would have invited you out for a cup of coffee."

There was that line again—that troubling line—"If we had known it was you." If we had known it was you we would have acted differently.

I.

I think I know now what was bothering me. Implied both in the spiritual and in the line from "Godspell" is that it's okay to have one set of behavioral standards for one group of people and another set of standards for another group. For special people, like Jesus, we are to be on our best behavior. But, for ordinary, run-of-the-mill people, we can act any old way.

That idea bothers me precisely because that's the way most of us determine our behavior. First we find out who we're dealing with, and then we decide how we're going to act. Special people deserve special behavior. Ordinary people do not. It's as simple as that!

How many cartoons have we all seen portraying some mischievous boys throwing snowballs and knocking the hats off passers-by? Then we see their chagrin when they discover that the offended party is the school principal, or a policeman, or a parent. The morality is clear, is it not? Knocking hats off people with snowballs is okay, unless it is somebody important.

The people for whom we reserve our best behavior are often those who have power or authority over us, or they are those who can do something for us, or they are those we admire or respect, or they are people we like. We are careful how we treat such people. We can be less careful with everyone else.

The pecking orders of every organization are interesting to observe. The classic arrangement is that the boss shouts at the employee, the employee shouts at the spouse, the spouse shouts at the child, the child kicks the dog. But the employee does not shout back at the boss for fear of his job. You see the pattern: our best behavior is reserved for special people.

When Jesus was giving his message about the last judgment, and the separating of the sheep from the goats, he was talking about a mind-set which has given us human beings trouble from the very beginning. Jesus knew that in the minds of his hearers the refusal to feed the hungry, clothe the naked, visit the sick and imprisoned is okay as long as we are not talking about someone important. That is what is implied in the statement, "If we had known it was you, we would have acted differently."

We have only to look around us to see how prevalent is that way of thinking and acting—one set of behavioral standards for the special people and another set of standards for everyone else. For example, it is generally acknowledged that in our society we have one level of justice for the nobodies and another level for the wealthy, the privileged, and the influential. Your chance for justice depends upon who you are. Doesn't that sound like a projection into the 21st century of the idea, "If we had known it was you, Jesus, we wouldn't have treated you so shabbily?"

Think about all the people in the world suffering from hunger, disease, illiteracy, abuse of all kinds. We don't like to think about such things. We'd rather close our eyes and hope such conditions will simply go away. But, of course, our reluctance to acknowledge and deal with such problems is symptomatic of their cause. We don't become agitated about such conditions precisely because, for the most part, the victims are the nameless, faceless, masses of the world. If it were my son or daughter suffering, I would want to know, and you can be sure I would do something. If it were Jesus suffering, not a one of us would stand idly by, because we Christians have strong feelings about Jesus. We would not tolerate any bad behavior toward him.

But do you hear what we are saying? Somewhere we have misplaced the concept of the worth and dignity of every human life, every human life. As the sons and daughters of the one Father, we are all brothers and sisters, and we are intended by God to act accordingly, to act like a family.

II.

Listen now: the Christian gospel says that we are not to divide people neatly into categories, the worthies over here and the unworthies over there. We are not to reserve our best behavior for special people and then dump our behavioral garbage on the nobodies of the world. Jesus sets before us some very high ethical standards. He says that we are not to act toward people as we think they deserve. And we are not to act simply according to how we feel. Instead, we are to deal with everyone according to grace, that is, according to unconditional love. Another way of saying that is: we are to act toward others as God acts toward us. God, in His love, gives us not what we deserve, but what we need. Thank God for that!

Now, you have heard all these words before. This is nothing new. But Jesus puts it even more graphically. According to Jesus, there are no "nobodies." There are no "unworthies." According to Jesus, we don't have to look carefully to see whether the person we are dealing with is Christ, because it always is! If Jesus means what he says, what he is telling us in clear language is that every human being we meet is Christ! Isn't that what it means: "Just as you did it to one of the least of these, my brothers and my sisters, you did it to me."

As special as Christ is to us Christians, every human being is to be equally special. And, how we act toward every human being is the way we act toward Christ. I can't think of a more profoundly disturbing, far-reaching ethical principle. Every person we meet is Christ and we are to act accordingly!

This vision of the worth and dignity of every human being has been one of the most powerful forces for good in human history. Whenever people's minds and hearts have been captured by it, significant change has taken place. One historian has claimed that four words brought about the virtual end to slavery in the world: "For whom Christ died." Once we take seriously the fact that every human being is one for whom Christ died, one who is loved by God, then we can't treat that person shabbily any more.

That's what Jesus was getting at when he laid down this radical principle. Listen to it again and try to wrap your mind around the greatness of it: "Just as you have done it to one of the least of these, my brothers and my sisters, you have done it to me." Jesus is identifying with the least, the poorest, the despised, the oppressed, the needy. You see them and you see Christ. You curse them and you curse Christ. You turn your back on them and you turn your back on Christ. You love and help them and you love and help Christ. Do you see the far reaching implications of what he is saying? If, when we look at any human being, we could see Christ and act accordingly, we just might begin to bring some healing and peace and justice to this battered and troubled world.

Of course, as always, we are not alone as we seek to be faithful to this vision. God is with us and will provide all that we need. God loves us and treats us as if we are special. Then He calls us to pass that loving along to others. And we can be certain that what God calls us to do He will help us to do.

In our last few minutes, let me tell you about some of the things that can happen when we begin to see Christ in those we meet. Try to get the feel of it if you can.

Mother Theresa of Calcutta is acknowledged to be a 20th century saint. She received the Nobel Peace Prize for her work among the poor and the oppressed of India. When she received the award, do you know what she said? She described her ministry simply as "seeing the face of

Christ in every person I meet, and then doing something beautiful for God." Do you hear it? "Just as you did it to one of the least of these, my brothers and my sisters, you did it to me." Mother Theresa understood.

Then, there was the shoeshine boy who did such a good job week after week that one of his customers asked him, "How is it that you are so conscientious about your work?" The little fellow looked up at him and said, "Mister, I'm a Christian, and I try to shine every pair of shoes as if Jesus were wearing them." The man never forgot those words. In fact, they led him to a new interest in the gospel and in reading the Bible. Eventually he committed his life to Christ. But he always credited his conversion to the boy who shined his shoes "as if Jesus were wearing them." "Just as you have done it to one of the least of these, my brothers and my sisters, you have done it to me."

I keep coming back again and again to the story of Conrad, the cobbler, as it is told by Edwin Markham. Conrad was a godly man, who sought to serve his Christ by the way he made and repaired shoes each day, and by the way he lived with his family and his neighbors through the week. One night he dreamed that Christ would visit his shop the next day. So, early in the morning, excitedly he went into the woods and gathered green boughs to decorate his shop for the Lord's coming. He prepared some food in case the Lord was hungry. And then he began to wait. He waited all morning, but the only visitor was an old man who came in asking for a place to rest. Conrad noticed that his shoes were old and worn, so he selected the finest pair of new shoes he had in the shop, put them on his feet, and sent the man on his way refreshed, because the old man had made contact with someone who cared.

Conrad waited for the Lord's coming through the afternoon, but the only person he saw was a woman struggling under a heavy load. He had compassion on her and invited her in to rest. She looked as if she had not had much to eat in awhile, so he gave her the food he had prepared for Christ. The woman found new strength and encouragement in Conrad's shop and she thanked him before continuing her journey.

He waited throughout the remaining afternoon, but no one else came. Just as night was falling, a lost child came wandering into his shop. Conrad struggled with what to do. If he left, he might miss the visitation. But the child was frightened, and he knew how worried the parents would be. So, he left his shop and returned the child to his waiting parents' arms. Conrad hurried back for fear that he would miss the coming of Christ. But, though he continued to wait, no one else came. Finally, in great disappointment, the old cobbler cried out,

"'Why is it Lord, that your feet delay, have you forgotten that this is the day?'

Then soft in the silence a voice he heard: 'Lift up your heart, for I have kept my word.
Three times I came to your friendly door; three times my shadow was on your floor.
I was the beggar with bruised feet; I was the woman you gave to eat;
I was the child on the homeless street.'"

Then Conrad remembered and understood as never before the words of Jesus: "Just as you have done it to one of the least of these, my brothers and my sisters, you have done it to me."

We can never again say, "If only we had known it was you." We cannot plead ignorance ever again. Wherever we are, whoever we meet, it is Christ, and we are to act accordingly.

Prayer: Father, forgive us when we treat Your children like nobodies instead of like Your special children, who they are. Give us the grace to look at the people we meet and see Christ in them. Then enable us to act lovingly and helpfully as we would act in His presence. Use such loving actions to bring a larger measure of peace and good-will to this world You love so much. In the Master's name we pray. Amen.

11.
Be Kind

Ephesians 4:31-32

Since before I can remember, I went to Vacation Bible School every summer. I loved Vacation Bible School and I have many fond memories of my experiences there. I remember rousing games of "Red Rover" in which the boys tried to impress the girls. I remember making first century houses out of clay. There were times when we dressed up in bath robes and re-enacted Biblical dramas. I remember spatter painting—I loved spatter painting! We would get a leaf or a flower or some other object and put it on a piece of paper. Then we would take a section of window screen, and, holding it over the paper, we would dip a toothbrush in paint and rub it across the screen, spattering the paint on the paper below. When the ink had dried, we removed the leaf or the flower, leaving its outline on the paper. In this way, even a non-artist like me could produce a lovely work of art. That is to say nothing of the spattered artwork on my clothes! But I loved it! There were caring people who gave generously of their time and energy to play games with us, teach us songs, tell us stories, and each day drill us on the memory verse—we always had a memory verse. I still have some of those verses, stored in my brain that I first learned at Vacation Bible School. "Make a joyful noise to the Lord, all the lands. Serve the Lord with gladness. Come before His presence with singing." "Be ye doers of the word, and not hearers only". And one came back into my mind recently which is the text of this sermon. Of course, all the memory verses were in King James English—it was the only Bible we had way back then! But it is just as fresh in my memory today as it was back then: "Be ye kind to one another, tender-hearted, forgiving one another." I'm glad that someone loved me enough to teach me that verse, because basic kindness is as important as anything else I know.

Probably we don't emphasize it enough. In our fast paced world, we talk a great deal about getting a good education, gaining as much academic mastery as possible. We talk about hard work, accomplishing a great deal in our chosen field, and earning as much as possible while we are at it. We talk about personal growth and development, about becoming the best we can be, physically, mentally, emotionally, spiritually. All of those are good things, worthy of aspiration. But we probably don't emphasize enough the importance simply of being kind to one another. While we are doing all the other things we do, while we are reaching for all the other goals to which we aspire, how do we treat people? Do we see people? Do we care about people? Do we act lovingly toward people?

We have all lamented a breakdown in basic civility. You know what I'm talking about: acting as if others don't matter. We all see it: guests in a motel talking and laughing 'til all hours, not thinking that other guests are trying to sleep. The person driving past other cars in a line wanting to get ahead, assuming that someone up ahead will let them in. People talking loudly in a restaurant as if they are the only patrons there. Taking a cell phone call in the middle of a movie or a concert. People breaking into the front of a line as if their business is more important than anyone else's. People dropping litter. Golfers neglecting to rake a bunker or repair a ball mark on a green. Not holding a door open for others. Common courtesy. I'll bet that a poor disposition has ruined more marriages than infidelity ever did. I'll bet that grouchiness and self-centeredness have spoiled more friendships and destroyed more careers than we know. And, at the same time, probably, more than anything else, the one thing that has endeared people to others is thoughtfulness and simple kindness. We admire people who are smart and competent, but we love those who are kind!

We see that at work in Jesus' life. He modeled kindness for all of us who follow him. When he fed crowds of people, it was because he was concerned about their hunger. He was motivated by kindness. When he healed the sick, it was not to show His power. In fact, he often asked people not to tell anyone. He was just moved to compassion because of his basic kindness. In that first century world, women and children didn't matter to most men. But Jesus included women in his inner circle and he rebuked the disciples when they tried to keep children away from him. Jesus was concerned about everybody. He had compassion for everybody: Jews, Samaritans, Gentiles, lepers, thieves, prostitutes, tax collectors—everybody! He expressed that compassion in kindness.

One of his best known parables, the parable of the Good Samaritan, is about one person helping another person in need. It's about human kindness.

It was so important to Jesus, in fact, that he made it the essential mark of authentic discipleship. He said, "This is how people will know that you are my disciples, if you have love for one another." Not if you believe all the right things. Not if you pray a lot. Not if you give a tithe of your income. Not if you worship in the right way. Those are all good things, but they are not the most important thing. According to Jesus, the way we show that we belong to Him is that we love one another, and that we act out our love by being kind to one another.

Of course, the reason we are to do that, and the reason we are able to do that is because of God's kindness toward us. The Bible says, "We love because He first loved us." Or, as our text from Ephesians puts it: "Be kind to one another, tenderhearted, forgiving one another, as God in Christ has forgiven you." So, God is kind to us, loving us, forgiving us, guiding us, strengthening us, blessing us, and we pass that on by being kind to one another. Hear me loud and clear—I can't say this often enough—we can't do it apart from God. It is God acting in us and through us that enables our kindness. But, clearly, if we do not act with kindness toward others, it is evidence that we have not received God's kindness toward us.

It is a constant source of sadness for me, to see people who claim to be followers of Jesus who are not very kind to others. They believe all the right things. They say all the right words. They espouse the right values and work for the right causes. They do so many right things, but do them in wrong ways. I remember a man who was a member of a former congregation. He had high standards. His ethics were impeccable. But he beat people over the head with his standards. People hated to see him coming. He was right about what he said and what he stood for, but so wrong in how he did it all. He was not very kind.

I love the prayer of the little girl: "God make the bad people good, and make the good people nice." There are too many religious people who are not very nice. Jesus, our model, stood for all the right things, but it was clear that he loved people, even bad people. And it was clear that his goal was not condemnation, but redemption. Even when he was saying hard things, he was still tenderhearted, and his basic kindness showed through.

Could the key to life really be that simple: that God loves us, so we can love one another? God is kind to us, so we can be kind to one another? Could it be that the most important things we do each day are to receive God's kindness and then to pass it on to others? To every person we meet in every thing we do? That's embarrassingly simple. But if I read the Bible correctly, that's what it's all about.

This sermon began forming in my heart and mind several years ago when I first saw the movie, "Wit," a Mike Nichols film, starring Emma Thompson. A great movie, not so much entertaining as disturbingly thought provoking. The movie is about Dr. Vivian Bearing, a first rate scholar, specializing in 17th century English literature, especially the poetry of John Donne. She had a biting wit which educated but also alienated her students. She had poured her life into becoming a scholar without peer. She was in control of her life, and she needed nothing, she thought, other than her scholarship and her career.

Then she was diagnosed with a rare form of ovarian cancer. She was confronted with a life situation for which all her scholarship had not prepared her. She no longer had all the answers. And she was no longer in control.

The usual treatments would not work, so she entered a teaching and research hospital, and agreed to experimental treatments. For eight months she underwent treatments which were painful and humiliating, and the outcome uncertain. She was no longer a teacher, but a subject for others to study. Her doctors were well versed in the latest treatments and technologies. They were very competent, and very detached and clinical. They would come into her room and talk about her instead of with her. She became, not Dr. Bearing, a real live human being with feelings and needs, but a certain disease being studied. They gave her the best medical treatment, but no human warmth. That was left to her nurse, Suzie, a wonderfully caring person.

In one of those moments when Vivian was talking out loud to herself, she said, "They always want to know more things—I always wanted to know more things, too. After all, I'm a scholar, or at least I was. We are discussing life and death, and not in the abstract. We are discussing my life and my death....nothing would be worse than a scholarly analysis." She goes on to say, "Now is the time for simplicity. Now is the time for, dare I say it—kindness." She concluded, "I thought being extremely smart would take care of it, but now I am being found out. I'm scared. O God, I want to hide!"

The experimental treatments weren't working. Her condition continued to deteriorate. Toward the end, she would go into and out of comas. One day while she was unconscious, the young research assistant came into the room, making rounds. The caring nurse began asking questions about "Why? Why?" Without even looking up from the chart he was examining, he replied: "You can't go around thinking about that meaning of life stuff all the time. You'd just go nuts." And with that, he left. The nurse responded by getting some lotion and gently massaging

Vivian's hands, who was not even aware of what she was doing. Her response to the "meaning of life stuff," as the doctor put it, was a simple act of kindness.

One day, toward the end of the movie, Vivian Bearing's teacher, the one under whom she had done her doctoral work, came to see her. She had not been aware of Vivian's sickness. She had come to town to visit a grandchild who was having a birthday. When she tried to call her former student, she learned that she was in the hospital, so she came by for a visit. Near death, Vivian was barely conscious, and in great pain. The elderly scholar tried to comfort her, but clearly was unsure of what to do. She said, "I'll recite something by Donne." Vivian said, "Nooooo!" Looking around, as if lost, the professor saw the books she had bought for her grandchild's birthday. So, she took a child's book from the bag, got up on the bed with Vivian, and held her in her arms while she read, "The Runaway Bunny." These two eminent scholars were comforted by a child's book about a mother bunny who assures her child that she will pursue him wherever he goes, because he is her little bunny. Of course, when you hear it with the ears of faith, you know the book is really about a God whose love will never let us go, wherever we are, and whatever we are going through. So, holding her tenderly, and reading the simple story of unfailing love, the professor helped Vivian drift into a peaceful sleep. What kindness!

In the final scene, the nurse had helped Vivian to accept her death. She helped her work through a decision to let death come. She wrote on the chart an order not to resuscitate. But when, mercifully, her heart stopped beating, the young doctor rushed in and began trying to revive her. When the nurse protested, the doctor said, "But she is research!" At that, the nurse physically got between Vivian and the doctor and made him stop. She allowed her to die in peace—the final kindness.

That movie drove me from complexity to simplicity. With all that we know, with all that we can do, does it all finally come down to this—is this the most important thing of all: are we kind to one another, as God is kind to us? At the end of the day, what you have accomplished and how much you have accumulated is not nearly as important as whom you have loved. The basic question is, "Are you kind?"

I want to conclude by sharing a true story, just as it was written by the person who had the experience. He wrote: "Twenty years ago, I drove a cab for a living. It was a cowboy's life, a life for someone who wanted no boss. What I didn't realize was that it was also a ministry. Because I drove the night shift, my cab became a moving confessional. Passengers climbed in, sat behind me in total anonymity, and told me about their lives. I encountered people whose lives amazed me, ennobled me, made me laugh and weep. But none touched me more than a woman I picked up late one August night.

When I arrived at 2:30 a.m., the building was dark except for a single light in a ground floor window. Under these circumstances, many drivers would just honk once or twice, wait a minute, and then drive away. But I had seen too many impoverished people who depended on taxis as their only means of transportation. Unless a situation smelled of danger, I always went to the door. "The passenger might be someone who needs my assistance," I responded to myself. So, I walked to the door and knocked. "Just a minute," answered a frail, elderly voice. I could hear something being dragged across the floor. After a long pause, the door opened. A small woman in her 80's stood before me. She was wearing a print dress and a pillbox hat with a veil pinned on it, like somebody out of a 1940's movie. By her side was a small nylon suitcase. The apartment looked as if no one had lived in it for years. All the furniture was covered with sheets. There were no clocks on the walls, no knickknacks or utensils on the counters. In the corner was a cardboard box filled with photos and glassware.

"Will you carry my bag out to the car?" she asked. I took the suitcase to the cab, then returned to assist the woman. She took my arm and we walked slowly toward the curb. She kept thanking me for my kindness. "It's nothing," I told her. "I just try to treat my passengers the way I would want my mother treated." "O, you're such a good boy," she said. When we got to the cab, she gave me an address, then asked, "Could you drive through downtown?" "It's not the shortest way," I answered quickly. "O, I don't mind," she said. "I'm in no hurry. I'm on my way to a hospice." I looked in the rear view mirror. Her eyes were glistening. "I don't have any family left," she continued. "The doctor says I don't have very long."

I quietly reached over and shut off the meter. "What route would you like me to take?" I asked. For the next two hours, we drove through the city. She showed me the building where she had once worked as an elevator operator. We drove through the neighborhood where she and her husband had lived when they were newlyweds. She had me pull up in front of a furniture warehouse that had once been a ballroom where she had gone dancing as a girl. Sometimes she'd ask me to slow in front of a particular building or corner and she would sit staring into the darkness, saying nothing. As the first hint of sun was creasing the horizon, she suddenly said, "I'm tired. Let's go now." We drove in silence to the address she had given me. It was a low building, like a small convalescent home, with a driveway that passed under a portico. Two orderlies came out to the cab as soon as we pulled up. They were solicitous and intent, watching her every move. They must have been expecting her. I opened the trunk and took the small suitcase to the door.

The woman was already seated in a wheelchair. "How much do I owe you?" she asked, reaching into her purse. "Nothing," I said. "You have to make a living," she answered. "There are other passengers," I responded. Almost without thinking, I bent over and gave her a hug. She held onto me tightly. "You gave an old woman a little moment of joy," she said. "Thank you".

I squeezed her hand, then walked into the dim morning light. Behind me, a door shut. It was the sound of the closing of a life. I didn't pick up any more passengers that shift. I drove aimlessly, lost in thought. For the rest of that day, I could hardly talk. What if that woman had gotten an angry driver, or one who was impatient at the end of his shift? What if I had refused to take the run, or had honked once, then driven away?

On a quick review, I don't think that I have ever done anything more important in my life."

Is that what it's about? At the end of the day, is it about kindness—first God's and then ours? Listen: "Be kind to one another, tenderhearted, forgiving one another, as God in Christ has forgiven you."

Prayer: Father, help us to love as we have been loved by You. Help us to reflect Your kindness to us simply by being kind. In Jesus' kind name we pray. Amen.

12.
Lord, Teach Us How To Pray

Luke 11:1-13

There is something within each of us that pulls us in the direction of God. There is a God-shaped empty place in us that will not be satisfied with anything less than God. Often we look for life in all the wrong places, only to discover that what Augustine said is true, "Thou hast made us for Thyself O God, and our hearts are restless 'til they find their rest in Thee."

God has given us the gift of prayer as the primary means by which we make connection with God and send our roots into the meaning of life. Let me give you my definition of prayer: Prayer is anything you do with a conscious awareness of God. It is what Brother Lawrence described as "practicing the presence of God." Whatever you are doing, you are aware of God, and open to His guidance and His strength.

Clearly, Jesus was a man of prayer. He was able to do the remarkable things he did only because he was plugged in to the source of meaning and power in life. Of course, I am talking about God. Prayer is where that contact took place. Jesus spent sizable blocks of time in intimate contact with God, through prayer. In prayer, Jesus was still and quiet and he experienced the "Godness" of God. He opened his life to the breezes of God's Spirit. He prayed daily as a matter of custom. But especially when he had a decision to make, a difficult task to do, or a cross to face, he would first spend time with God in prayer, and then go to do what he had to do. The disciples knew that prayer was the source of Jesus' power. That's why they asked Him, "Lord, teach us how to pray." Today, that's our request as well.

I.

To begin with, if we are to learn about prayer from Jesus, we must see that, for Him, prayer was not sporadic. It was not hit and miss, occasional, for emergencies only. No, for Jesus, prayer was a matter of daily discipline. If we are to gain any satisfaction from our prayer life, ours must be a matter of discipline as well.

There must be a definite time set aside each day for prayer. Certainly that is not the only time we pray. Our goal is to reach the place, as Paul put it, when we pray without ceasing; that is, we are aware of God wherever we are, whatever we are doing. But that consciousness begins with daily, disciplined prayer. That becomes the fertile soil out of which all other prayer grows.

One reason daily discipline is so important is that prayer, like anything worthwhile, takes practice. Early on, you probably won't be very comfortable with it. But you've got to stay with it, trusting that God is there wanting to make contact with you, even if you are not aware of Him at first. In my imagination, like the cellular phone commercial, I hear God saying, "Can you hear me now? Good!"

I don't know why we have thought that prayer is supposed to be automatic and easy. Few interpersonal relationships are. Most relationships take work. We must invest the time necessary to get to know one another. It takes time and it takes work. Prayer is like that, too. It takes time for God and us to get to know one another and how best to communicate with one another.

I know that most people give up too quickly. There is a story about H.G. Wells, that when he was a young man he prayed hard for something to happen. It didn't, so he said, "All right for you, Mister God, I won't bother you again." And he didn't. That was the end of his prayer life.

The world is full of people who say, "I've tried prayer and it didn't work." I've always wondered why we give up so quickly on something as important as prayer, while we invest significant amounts of time, money, and effort on enterprises far less important.

I've never seen a person sit down at a bridge table, bid the hand correctly and make a grand slam the first time out. But neither have I seen people make a mistake and say, "I've tried bridge and I can't play it, so I quit." No, they work at it, often for years. They read books, talk with experienced players, and they practice. And, by working at it, they improve.

I've never seen a person go to the golf course and play a round in par the first time out. I know I didn't. I dribbled the ball off the tee and sliced it all over the course, that is, when I managed to make contact with the ball at all. But I saw that there were people who could play the game, so I began to work at it. I'm still not very good, but I am better than I was. I know that improvement is possible with practice.

I know that the analogy holds for prayer. My early attempts at prayer were not very satisfying either. But I saw that other people I admired and respected were people of prayer. I saw what it produced in their lives. I wanted to be in touch with whatever it was that produced such strength, beauty, and authenticity in their lives. So, I continued to pray. And I am convinced that continuous, meaningful contact with God must grow out of a regular, disciplined time set aside for God's exclusive use.

Understand that such time in God's presence is not optional; it is essential for the life of faith. Using Brother Lawrence's definition, "practicing the presence of God," like all practice, it must be regular. There was a concert pianist who said, "If I miss practice for one day, I know it. If I miss two days, the critics know it. If I miss a week, everyone knows it." Practice. Discipline. That's essential to prayer.

What we want to happen during our times of prayer is that we simply will be still, and open, and there experience the reality of God. We will allow His love to wash over us like the waves of the sea. We will allow His strength to blow upon us like the wind blows through a field of wheat. We will allow God to tell us who He is, who we are, and what we are called to be and do for Him and for one another.

It is true that we can find God and worship God in nature, in music, in art, and in other people. We can see God and encounter God in all of the events of daily life. But I am convinced that unless we make time for God in a regular, disciplined life of prayer, we will not develop the sensitivity necessary to see Him and to acknowledge Him in all these other ways.

In a previous sermon, I shared the quote, "God always waits on His regular customers first." That doesn't mean that God plays favorites. It means that God is always available, always seeking to make contact with us and give us the best gifts of life. But only God's "regular customers" have developed the sensitivity necessary to see God, to hear God, and to respond to God.

This means that we must not wait until we feel like it to pray. No, we pray daily as a matter of faith, as a matter of trust, believing that God will meet us in prayer and do something good for us. We trust that and we act on that, even at those times when we do not have religious goose bumps, even when, at the feeling level, we aren't sure God is there. It's a matter of regularity, a matter of discipline.

II.

Now let me make some very practical suggestions about the time you set aside for prayer. First, get comfortable. Assume whatever physical posture that will make you most open to God. Picture yourself, your whole being, as in the hands of God. One great man of prayer thinks of himself as a piece of driftwood being carried on the waves of a powerful and limitless ocean, except, to him, the ocean is the love of God.

Second, think of God as being present, really present, as real as any of the material things in your presence. Some people place a chair nearby and picture God as being in the chair. Do whatever you have to do to think of God as really present.

Third, it may be helpful to read something to help you tune in. Scripture is good, perhaps something from the Psalms, or some devotional material. Poetry is sometimes helpful. This is our way of taking down the barriers between us and God, helping us focus our attention, and making us available to God.

Fourth, be honest. Martin Luther's first rule of prayer was, "Don't lie to God!" A major barrier to reality in prayer is that we tend to stand outside ourselves and wonder how we look and sound to God. We try to manufacture a "prayer language" that sounds to us like we think a prayer should sound. The fact is, God doesn't care how we sound. He just wants us to be ourselves in His presence—to be real—so that He can love us and give us what we need. Please know that God wants to meet YOU in prayer, not some pious image of yourself that you try to project. God loves us just as we are, so we are free to be who we are in prayer. So, be real, be honest.

For the next few minutes I want to talk about the content of prayer. Part of our prayer time will be verbal. Not necessarily speaking aloud, but we will formulate our thoughts into words and phrases and offer them to God. In addition to that, part of our prayer time will be spent listening—and I want to talk more about that a little later. Keith Miller has suggested a pretty good formula for the time we offer words and thoughts to God. In order for prayer to be balanced, and include all that should be included, Keith says that most prayer should involve at least four parts, beginning with the letters in Acts: A-C-T-S.

First, there is Adoration, a time when we are still and allow God to be God. During this part of our prayer time we are to center our thoughts completely upon God. It might be helpful to visualize God as we have come to know Him in Jesus. But our attention must be upon God and not upon ourselves. I once heard a great man of prayer say,

"Prayer is not primarily a hall of mirrors where we look at ourselves, but an Upper Room where we are with Christ." Adoration.

Then, there is Confession, a time when we are honest with God about ways we have failed Him, our neighbors, and ourselves. We confess and humbly ask for forgiveness. Now, be specific in this. Don't just confess in general, saying, "God forgive me for my sins." God's response to such a prayer might be, "Such as..." When our confession is specific, God's forgiveness will also be specific. The response always is, "You are forgiven!"

Third, there is a time of Thanksgiving, a time for expressing gratitude for the many gifts of God's love. Take plenty of time to count your blessings and to acknowledge God as the source of all good gifts. You know, there is real healing in thanksgiving. To acknowledge God's generosity helps to save us from depression, from self-centeredness, from smallness of spirit. "Count your blessings, name them one by one, and it will surprise you what the Lord has done." Thanksgiving.

Finally, according to Keith Miller, this part of our prayer time should conclude with Supplication, that is, offering concerns up to God, making requests of God. I believe that there is power in prayer. And God has supremely honored us by allowing us to participate in the good things He is doing in the world through prayer. God takes us so seriously that there are some things God will not do without our participation in prayer. We are invited to pray for our family, our friends, our church, our nation, our world. And, as we pray, energy is released to encourage certain things to happen. It is well documented: there is power in prayer to change things.

There are two things we are to learn about prayer from Jesus' prayer in the Garden of Gethsemane. First, Jesus prayed, "Father, if it is possible, let this cup pass from me." We are invited to pray for specific things, but as Jesus recognized, some things are not possible. We don't know in advance what is possible and what is not, so we pray. Most importantly, in Jesus' prayer in the garden, we are introduced to the highest moment of prayer. It is when we can pray and mean, as did Jesus, "Nevertheless, not my will, but Thine be done." The bottom line is, if we are people of faith, we want what God wants, because we know that what God wants is always what is best for us. So, subject to those two modifications, we are to make our requests known to God. And, when we pray earnestly, persistently, powerful things can happen.

Now, as important as it is to have that time when we formulate words and thoughts and offer them to God, probably the largest portion of our prayer time should be spent in Listening. As someone has pointed out,

"God gave us two ears and only one mouth, so we are to spend twice as much time in listening as in talking." I like the story of the little girl who was saying her prayers at night. She finished what she had to say, but did not say, "Amen." Impatiently, her mother said, "Why don't you say, 'Amen' so you can go to sleep?" The little girl said, "I was just waiting to see if God had anything to say to me." She had the right idea.

What do we listen for? Well, if we are waiting for the kind of voice that could be recorded on a tape recorder, we might have a long wait. The "still, small voice" the Bible talks about is more the sense of a presence, not ourselves, but Someone. It may involve a sense of well being, closely akin to the experience of being held. Perhaps we feel an "oughtness," I ought to do this, or I ought not do that. Maybe we have been wrestling with a problem, trying to make a decision, and suddenly there comes a kind of clarity. Perhaps we have been carrying around a load of guilt, or have been weighted down with worry, and now there comes a sense of forgiveness, a feeling of peace. Something like that, I think, is the voice of God. And, if there is ever any confusion about whether or not it is God, just measure it by Jesus. If what you are hearing, sensing, or feeling looks and sounds like Jesus, you can be sure it is God.

Read the gospels and you will see that Jesus did not believe much in long prayers. His model prayer, the Lord's Prayer, is really very brief. And he chided those who thought they would be heard because they prayed long prayers. No, Jesus did not believe in long prayers, but He did believe in long praying. He sometimes spent days, even weeks in prayer. But most of that time He spent in silence, allowing God to shape His spirit and mold His life.

If prayer is what I think it is—if prayer is a time exposure of the soul to God, with the primary purpose being to allow something of God's Spirit to be impressed upon our spirits, then a great deal can happen in prayer. The key is to keep at it. Make prayer an important part of your everyday routine. By doing that, you may reach the place where it is such a smooth transition between that time set apart for prayer and the rest of the day, that all of life becomes a prayer and you become aware of God at almost every moment and in virtually every place.

The one thing I am sure of is that if you take prayer seriously, it will change your life. When I was a boy, my mother hung a plaque on my bedroom wall. It said, "Prayer changes things." At that time, I didn't understand that. I'm not sure I even believed it. But I believe it now. Often prayer is able to change the situation in which we find ourselves. But always prayer is able to change the person who is praying. In prayer we receive love and guidance and strength. What else do we need?

A poet said it like this:

"Speak to Him thou, for He hears,
And spirit with Spirit can meet;
Closer is He than breathing,
And nearer than hands and feet."

God is here. Wherever we are, God is there. There is so much that He wants to give us. The miracle occurs when we make contact, through prayer.

Prayer: Loving Father, we do feel Your tug at our hearts, and we do want to be with You. So, we echo the prayer of the disciples so long ago: "Lord, teach us how to pray." Amen.

13
Jesus' Forty Days, and Ours

Matthew 4:1-11

Matthew, Mark, and Luke all begin their stories of the adult Jesus at the Jordan River, where he is baptized by his cousin John. In baptism, Jesus identifies with us, and with all people everywhere. And, there, at the baptism, God said, "This is my beloved son in whom I am well pleased." At the beginning of the story, the gospel writer wants to make it clear who this is he is telling about: this is Jesus, the son of God! What a powerful beginning to the story!

Jesus knew, as he must have known for some time, that God was calling him to a special mission. Now was the time to begin it. So, he went into the wilderness to sort it all out, to clarify the nature of God's call. He stayed in that wilderness, fasting and praying for 40 days (that's where we get the 40 days of Lent.) And, his time in the wilderness was much like the 40 years Israel spent in the wilderness on their way to the promised land. During that time, both Israel and Jesus were tempted, or, put to the test. And, they emerged from the test even stronger in faith, not in spite of the testing, but in large measure because of it.

Jesus went into the wilderness because he wanted to leave the world of many voices. He wanted to hear the One voice, the voice of God. What he discovered was that even in that remote wilderness there was more than one presence, and there was more than one voice. There always is. It was up to Jesus and it is up to us to sort out the many voices we hear. To focus on the One voice that is the source of truth, the source of strength, the source of life. The ultimate question is: in the presence of many voices calling to us, enticing us, and tempting us, to what voice will we listen?

Jesus was there without any human companions, so he must have told this story to the disciples later. He must have considered it to be a watershed moment in his life. If God was calling him to be the Messiah, the question was, what kind of Messiah was he to be? The people wanted a Messiah like David, the greatest of the Hebrew kings. They wanted a Messiah who would recruit an army, defeat the Romans, and bring back the good old days of peace, pride, and prosperity. Would Jesus listen to the voice of the people and attempt to do all those things? It occurs to me that sometimes the voice of the majority is the same as the voice of the devil.

I'm convinced that at least part of the temptation, the testing, was to listen to the voice of the people and to become that kind of Messiah. It would have been far easier and more popular for Jesus simply to go along, and to become an earthly king. But, that's not the choice he made. Listening to the voice of God, he rejected the urging of the people and embraced an image given by Isaiah in the Exile. Jesus sensed that God was calling him to be a suffering servant, one who would win people not by force, but by the redemptive power of a love that loves enough to suffer. Jesus was called to the way of the cross.

I think that became clear to Jesus there in the wilderness, and the time of testing was a part of that clarifying process. It will be a great thing if something like that can happen to us during our 40 days of Lent. It will be a great thing if we can become clear about who we are as children of God, clear about what God is calling us to do, and clear about our commitment to do it!

Let's look for a few moments at the setting for Jesus' temptation/ testing experience. Tradition tells us that, after Jesus' baptism in the Jordan River, he went west, toward Jerusalem, into the Wadi Qelt. That's a real wilderness. There would not have been anyone else around for miles. And the devil used the setting as a source of temptation. I have stood there in that wilderness and tried to imagine what Jesus must have seen and experienced. Under foot, there are stones worn smooth by thousands of years of running water, stones that look very much like loaves of bread. To the left and to the right, there are the rugged crags of high mountains that must have reminded Jesus of the pinnacle of the Temple. And, looking back, toward the river, there was the splendor of one of Herod's magnificent palaces, reminding him of the great kingdoms of the world.

It's fascinating to me that the same setting, the same event can be used either for inspiration or for temptation, depending upon who is doing the interpretation. Jesus would often use natural settings as sources of inspiration. He would see a farmer planting seed, and he would begin a parable, "Behold a sower went forth to sow..." He would see a shepherd tending his flock, and Jesus would say, "I am the good shepherd, I know my sheep, and my sheep know my voice." Jesus would call attention to a vineyard and say, "I am the vine, you are the branches," using the setting as a source of inspiration.

But here, the devil points to things around them and uses them to tempt, to defile. Remember, Jesus had just come from one of the high moments of his life. There, at his baptism, he had heard God say, "This is my beloved son in whom I am well pleased." A great moment of inspiration! But as soon as he got into the wilderness, the devil took that time of inspiration and turned it around, planting seeds of doubt. He began the temptation by saying, "If...if...if you are the son of God, do this, do that—if! If you are the son of God, then prove it!" And, if he was the son of God, and if he was to be the kind of Messiah the people wanted, the things he was tempted to do seemed reasonable, even desirable!

If Jesus did the three things he was tempted to do, those things would hold great promise for an earthly kingdom: bread for him, and for the world, political control of all nations, a spectacular feat to gain the attention and the affection of the masses. Why not? Why not? If that is what you want to accomplish.

Here in the first days of Jesus' ministry, he shows us something important: temptation is real. And it comes to all of us. It came to Jesus, and it comes to us, every one of us. And, this time in the wilderness was not the last of Jesus' struggles with it. You remember that Peter tempted him to reject the way of the cross, and Jesus said to him, "Get behind me, Satan!" And, that struggle in the Garden of Gethsemane—the struggle so intense that sweat appeared on his brow like great drops of blood—Jesus was tempted again to reject the cross and to say "No" to what God was calling him to do. No, Jesus had recurring temptations, and we will too, as long as we live.

I've never been able to believe in a red devil, with horns, and a tail, and a pitchfork. That stereotype is too easily dismissed. I don't care whether you call him or it the devil, Satan, Lucifer, Beelzebub, the deceiver, the tempter. I don't care whether you personalize it or depersonalize it. But, whoever or whatever it is, we have to deal with it. We know it all too well, don't we? There is something at work in the world and in us that tempts us to be less than we know we ought to be. There is something that tempts us to move away from God toward the dark side. Paul knew about it. That's why he said that we have a battle on our hands. We'd better put on the whole armor of God, so that we can stand against the wiles of the devil. Luther knew about it. That's why he wrote in his hymn, "His craft and power are great, and armed with cruel hate, on earth is not his equal." However you picture it, you had better take it seriously, as Jesus did.

I don't know about you, but in my wrestling with the devil, I have learned how clever he is. He knows where my weak places are. He knows what buttons to push. He knows how to place those devilish rationalizations in my mind. You've heard the whispers in the ear, I know. "No one will know—just this once won't hurt—you're entitled— besides, everyone is doing it." Have you heard those whispers? And, the most diabolical one of all: "Generally speaking, this doesn't work out very well, but it won't happen to you, the negative consequences won't happen to you. You're the exception!" He knows our weaknesses, doesn't he?

But not only does he tempt us at our weak places, he can even use our strengths to weaken us. I heard a pastor confess it. He was a superb preacher, took it seriously, and worked at it. One night he was working on the sermon for the following Sunday. He little son came in and asked his daddy to come tuck him in. The father told him to get into bed and he would come in a few minutes to give him a goodnight kiss and tuck him in. But then, he became engrossed in his preparation, and much later, he remembered the promise. He went into his son's bed room only to discover that the little fellow was already asleep. That story breaks my heart, because it has a familiar ring to it. His passion to be a good preacher—a good thing—had tempted him that night to be a bad father. Do you hear it? The tempter even turns our strengths against us if we are not careful.

Well, if temptation is real and if we will be wrestling with it all our lives, how best to deal with it? Let's look at how Jesus did it. There, in the wilderness, every time he was tempted, he quoted scripture. And, don't miss the fact that all of the scriptures he quoted were from the Exodus. When facing his own struggles in the wilderness, he looked back and remembered Israel's struggles in their wilderness.

That should give us a clue as to what scripture is. To quote scripture is not like rubbing Aladdin's lamp to produce a miracle. It's not like holding a cross out in front of a threatening vampire. No, it works like this, I think. Listen now, because I'm about to say something important. To quote scripture is to remember. It is to recall how God has been faithful and dependable in times past. It is to recall how God's grace and strength has always been sufficient for our every need. And, as we remember, God Himself comes to us and gives us what we need to resist temptation. God comes and gives us what we need to cope. And God uses that experience to make us stronger and more faithful followers of Jesus. Scripture is not just the record of what God said and did long ago. It is the means by which we open ourselves to Him so that He can do it again right here, right now!

That's what happened to me. When I was diagnosed with prostate cancer, at the instant the doctor pronounced the "C" word, there popped into my mind some verses of scripture that I had not thought about for over fifty years. I know my mother had placed them there because they were from the King James translation. Here are the words: "Thou wilt keep him in perfect peace whose mind is stayed on Thee." (Isaiah 26:3) Instantly I thought of those words, after not hearing them for over fifty years. They had simply been filed away there for the time when I would need them. In the weeks following, whenever I thought about cancer, I would think of those words. They were the last words in my mind when I went under the anesthesia. They were the first words in my mind when I awoke. And, throughout the whole process, God freed me from anxiety and fear.

Do you understand? I wasn't just remembering some words. I was remembering that God's grace is always sufficient—always has been, always will be. And, as I remembered, God Himself was there, and He kept His promise, "Thou wilt keep him in perfect peace, whose mind is stayed on Thee."

There in the wilderness, Jesus was tempted by the devil. The devil called to him, pleaded with him, made promises to him, told him lies. It was tempting. What did Jesus do with it? He quoted scripture and changed the channel. You see, that's the choice always open to us. We can either continue to listen to the persuasions of the devil, and as we listen, we give them more power. Or, we can change the channel and tune in to God. That's what Jesus did when he quoted scripture. He tuned the devil out, and tuned God in.

I've said it before: the mind cannot focus on more than one thing at a time. We have a choice as to our focus. When we are focusing on God, we cannot at the same time be listening to the tempter. When the devil comes with his persuasive arguments, we can just do as Jesus did, take the remote, click on God, and change the channel.

Let me give some examples. When someone has hurt us, and we are tempted to become angry, we allow that experience to damage the relationship. If we continue to rehearse the hurt, we give it more power, and the situation becomes worse. But, if we change our focus to God, allow Him to come and remind us of the number of times He has forgiven us, perhaps our hard heart will begin to melt and we receive the power to love and forgive, and healing begins.

When we are tempted to compromise with our own values and thus become less than our best, the more we focus on the situation, the more the tempter shows us how to rationalize and gives us "good reasons" for doing the thing we know we should not do. But, if we focus on God, God comes and reminds us that we were made for something better than that. We are a child of God and the very best in life comes to us when we act like it.

When we have been diagnosed with an illness, the more we concentrate on the illness, the more power we give it, and the tempter uses that to weaken our resistance. But, if we will focus on God, God comes and gives us strength and courage to resist, and frees all of the body's recuperative powers to fight back.

You get the point. We need not be in this struggle alone. When we are tempted to be less than our best, when we are tempted to despair, to give in, or to give up, turn to the scriptures. Remember who God is and what He has done, remember that God's grace and strength have been sufficient in the past, remember all of that and then God will come and do it again, right here, right now.

Where did Jesus go from his wilderness experience? Instead of being weakened by it, he was strengthened by it. He immediately left the wilderness, called his disciples, and got at the task to which God had called him. He was very clear now about who he was and what he was to do. He was God's son, and he was to be about his Father's business.

I love the way Matthew closes the wilderness story. After Jesus had changed channels, after Jesus had turned his back on Satan and turned toward God, the Bible says that angels came and ministered to him. Isn't that beautiful? Angels came and ministered to him. Do you suppose Jesus was remembering that when he said, "Seek first the Kingdom of God—the centrality of God—put that first, and then everything else that you need will be yours as well."

Angels came and ministered to him. That is a beautiful way of saying that God was there, God was real, and God's grace and strength were sufficient.

I remember a poem that says it. Listen:

> "At the heart of the cyclone, tearing the sky,
> and flinging the clouds and the towers by
> is a place of central calm.
> So, here in the roar of mortal things,
> I have a place where my spirit sings...
> in the hollow of God's palm."

You place yourself there, and you will be equal to all the demands of life.

Prayer: We know now where to turn, our Father, when we are tempted by voices other than Yours. We remember who we are, whose we are, and we remember all that You have done in the past by Your grace and strength. Then we place our lives in your loving hands, knowing that there, we are secure. Give us the grace to do just that, as Jesus did, in whose name we pray. Amen.

14.
It Was For Us

Luke 23:33-34

There is a Lenten hymn whose words have special meaning for me:

"There is a green hill far away, beyond the city wall,
Where the dear Lord was crucified, who died to save us all.
We may not know, we cannot tell what pains he had to bear,
But we believe it was for us he hung and suffered there."

That has been the affirmation of the Christian faith for 2,000 years now, that although the crucifixion of Jesus took place a long time ago, at a location far removed from where we are, somehow in a profound way it was for us.

In what sense was it for us? Well, in order to deal with that question, we've got to go back to the beginning. The Bible says that in the beginning God created. He created everything that is. And, the supreme act of creation was the creation of human beings. The Psalmist said of us, "You have made him a little lower than the angels, and have crowned him with glory and honor." God created us very much like himself: able to think, to make value judgments, to make choices, to enter into relationships or not. God wanted creatures much like himself, creatures whom he can love, creatures who will respond to his love by loving him in return.

James Weldon Johnson expressed that beautifully in his poem, "The Creation." He wrote:

"And God stepped out on space. And he looked around and said, 'I'm lonely. I'll make me a world.'" So he did. He created the mountains and the rivers, the oceans and the dry land. He created the world with all its living things. And God looked on all that he had made and said, "That's good!" But, after looking at that world, God said, "I'm lonely still." So God thought and thought 'til he thought, "I know. I'll make me a man!" And so he did."

"I'm lonely," God said. Perhaps you think that word, "lonely" is too human a word. But it comes as close as any word I know to describing why we are here. If God is love, and if love is not complete until it is expressed, that comes close to explaining it. God wanted to complete himself by creating us, and loving us, intending for us to respond to his love by loving him in return.

But God, in his wisdom, knew that love is real only when it is given freely. So, as soon as God created us, He set us free. Get that! We were created to live in a loving, trusting, obedient relationship with God. But so badly does God want our relationship with Him to be real, that as soon as He created us, He set us free to say "No" to that relationship. He set us free to turn our backs on Him and to live our lives as if God doesn't even exist, if we insist upon doing that. Now I don't fully understand that, but I surely do respect that—a God who takes us that seriously, to set us free!

I have to tell you my favorite story about freedom. A family went into a restaurant to eat: a mother, father, and young son. A waitress came to the table, took the order of the mother and the father, and then turned to the son. "What'll you have?" she asked. "I want a hot dog," he said. Both parents said rather emphatically, "No hot dog!" But the waitress was not listening to the parents. "What do you want on your hot dog?" she asked. The boy broke into a big grin and said, "Ketchup, lots of ketchup, and bring me a glass of milk!" "Coming up!" she said, and turned to go place the orders. The little boy followed her with his eyes, open wide in amazement. When the waitress had disappeared behind the swinging doors of the kitchen, he turned to his parents and said, "You know what? She thinks I'm real!"

I don't know where that story belongs in the realm of family discipline. I'm not going to get into that. But there is no doubt where that story belongs in Christian theology: dead center, right at the heart. Because God thinks we are real. We are not puppets on a string being manipulated by divine power. We are not actors on a stage, going through some motions that have been choreographed in advance, speaking some lines written by some unseen playwright. No, we are real people making real choices, with everything at stake in the choices we make. God has placed us in a world where we can order hot dogs, whether they are good for us or not, and if we order them we will get them, together with all the side effects that come with them. We are real!

But that first story in the Bible accurately portrays the down side of all of that. From the very beginning we human beings used our freedom to say "No" to God and to go our own way. There it is in the story. And, by the way, the story is not just about a man and a woman named Adam and Eve. It's the universal story. It's the story of your life and mine. Here it is: God created us and placed us in a good world with everything we need to make life good. There is just one stipulation: God must be God! Of course, that is the very rule we refuse to obey. From the beginning there has been that rebellious streak in us. We want to do our own thing in our own way. We want to be God! In the Adam and Eve story that was acted out over the forbidden fruit. But if it had not been that it would have been something else. And the consequence of Adam and Eve's disobedience was that they had to leave the garden. That's just a poetic way of saying that they became separated from God, and separated from life as it was intended to be. Simply put, that is what the Bible calls sin. Sin, basically, is the condition of being separated from God.

So, that is why life has gone wrong. We were created to live in a loving, trusting relationship with God. But we used our freedom to turn from that. And, when we refuse to allow God to be God, when we put someone or something else at the center of life, then it all goes wrong.

Now, what is God to do about all of that? I suppose God could use his power to threaten us. He could use his strength to coerce us. But that wouldn't work. God knows us too well to bully us. That would never accomplish God's purpose. You can't force someone to love you.

But God will never give up on us. The story of the Bible is the story of a God who, century after century, keeps pursuing us. He has reached out to us with prophets, priests, messengers. He has tugged at our hearts by his Spirit. He has whispered in our ear again and again, "You are mine, don't you know that? I love you. Won't you come home to me where you belong?" And, finally, when everything was prepared, God took a bold new step. He made his last, best effort to get through to us in the life, death, and resurrection of his son, Jesus. Through Jesus, God has spoken to us in the persuasive language of love.

When we read about Jesus in the gospels, we must realize that much of what Jesus said had been said before. His summary of the meaning of all the Jewish scriptures was a quote. But there are at least two emphases we see in Jesus that are new. First, in Jesus we are introduced to a seeking God—not a God who is in hiding and must be found, not a reluctant God who must be persuaded to love and forgive us. No, not that. In Jesus we are introduced to a God who actively seeks us out in all our favorite hiding places in order to draw us to himself and to give us the gift of abundant life. He is the good shepherd who goes out in the night seeking the one sheep who is lost. He is the father out there on the road, running to greet his son coming home, arms of love and welcome spread wide. That's God, according to Jesus, the One who seeks us.

But, even more significantly, Jesus introduces us to a vulnerable God, a suffering God. Especially at the cross we meet a God who loves enough to suffer for those who are loved. Earlier in history we were told about a powerful God, a righteous God, a provident God, even a loving God, but this is something new. Paul called it a stumbling block, a scandal. Here is a God who loves enough to suffer.

Crucifixion was a terrible way to die. It was such a cruel death that it was reserved for the worst enemies of Rome. Typically it was days before death would come, mercifully bringing an end to the shame and pain. And often the bodies were left there for weeks or months as a warning to others who might be tempted to oppose Rome. Death was not caused by loss of blood. It was caused by exhaustion, dehydration, asphyxiation. The body was placed on a kind of wooden saddle so the flesh of hands and feet would not be torn by the weight of the body. But after hours of hanging there the chest would collapse and make it difficult to breathe. And the one on the cross would have to choose whether or not to lift himself up by his hands in order to breathe, causing excruciating pain, or whether simply to hang there, unable to breathe. Finally death came by asphyxiation. Jesus' death came in a relatively short time. But just look at what was happening during that time. He cried out in pain and thirst. He prayed. He gave his mother over to the care of his friend, John. He made a promise to one of the thieves. He forgave his executioners. And finally, he commended his spirit to God, from whom it had come.

Never was a man treated more unjustly, more cruelly than was Jesus. All he had wanted to do was to love them. All he had wanted to do was to give them life at its best. But you see what they did to him. How would you expect him to respond to all of that? With a curse? With a threat? With a vow to get even? Such a response would be understandable.

But that is not what Jesus did. Through it all, he trusted his Father. Through it all, he continued to love. And, amazingly, he looked down at the very ones who nailed him to the cross and prayed for them, and for us. He prayed, "Father, forgive them, for they do not know what they are doing."

There at the cross we see an amazing kind of love. We see a love that absorbs wrong, that bears wrong, and bears it in such a way that it takes it away. The good news is that "As far as the East is from the West, so far has he removed our transgressions from us." "Father, forgive them."

Now I don't fully understand that kind of forgiving love, but I have experienced it. And I tell you, it's the most liberating, the most exhilarating, the most life-giving experience I know! At this moment I know that I am loved. I am forgiven. I am secure in the Father's care. My life is of infinite worth. I know that, I know that because I am one for whom Christ has died. And so are you!

I believe that is at the heart of divine strategy. We have been made in such a way that we cannot be reached in our depths by threat, by coercion, by force. No, God can get through to us and bring us back to himself only through the amazing, persuasive power of suffering love.

I remember reading somewhere about a man who had tried everything he knew to try to experience the best in life. He had looked in all the wrong places. And still there was that emptiness, that anxiety, that restlessness at the center of his life. He was so tired of playing games. He was so disappointed in all the failures he had experienced. Nothing seemed to work. Finally, almost in desperation, he had an encounter with the man on the cross and became a new man in Christ. From that moment on, everything was new. Life became the good gift God intended it to be.

When asked to describe his experience, he said something like this: "I just came to Jesus. And, much to my amazement, he didn't scold me. He knew I had been scolded enough. And he didn't give me any advice either. He knew I had had plenty of that. He just put his arms around my neck and loved me. And when the sun rose, I was a new man."

That's what happened to me when I met that man on the cross, that man with his suffering, forgiving love.

> "We may not know, we cannot tell what pains he had to bear,
> But we believe it was for us he hung and suffered there."

It's true. Jesus' death was in some profoundly moving way, for us. Through that experience God's love reaches out to us. And when it finally gets through to us, when it finally touches us in the deep places of our heart, it saves us, and we are never again the same.

Prayer: Loving Father, we are so very grateful for your amazing grace which comes to us from the cross. We are not worthy of it, but we are so very grateful for it. Help us now to know that we are of infinite worth because we are those for whom Christ has died. We share now in the pain and sorrow of his death, in the assurance that we will also share in the joy and power of his resurrection. In the name of Christ, we pray. Amen.

15.
Sing the Resurrection Song

Mark 16:1-8

None of the four gospels tells the whole story of the crucifixion and resurrection of Jesus. We have to read all four to get the full picture. The well known "seven last words from the cross" for example, are not found in any one gospel account. In order to hear all seven words, you've got to read all four of the gospels. And, accounts of the resurrected Jesus' appearances to his followers are spread throughout the four as well.

While all the gospels are important, probably each of us has his or her favorite. I imagine that most of us like the resurrection accounts in Matthew or in John. Of course, the story in Luke has its moments too. Who can forget the two followers of Jesus meeting him, but not recognizing him, on the road to Emmaus. After recognizing him, and recalling the experience later, they described it like this: "Were not our hearts burning within us while he was talking to us on the road!" What a beautiful way of talking about our experience with Christ— "the burning heart." Probably that's where the hymn writer got the inspiration for the words: "You ask me how I know he lives. He lives within my heart."

In comparing the gospel accounts of the resurrection, though, probably most people like the story in Mark the least. It is the briefest and gives fewer details than the others. But the thing that makes us most uncomfortable, I imagine, is the abrupt ending. Many Biblical scholars believe that the original gospel of Mark ended with verse 8 of the 16th chapter. The rest was added later, they believe. I suppose that's one reason I like the account in Mark. It ends with the words: "So they went out and fled from the tomb, for terror and amazement had seized them; and they said nothing to anyone, for they were afraid." And, just like that, it ends.

Why in the world would Mark have ended it like that? Jesus was resurrected. The women ran away in fear and said nothing to anyone. And the gospel ends right there. Why?

Some have called Mark, "the unfinished gospel." It ends so abruptly, and it ends not with joy and celebration, but with amazement and fear. Unfinished. I guess that's why I like it. Because it's up to us now to finish it. Jesus has been raised from the dead. He has won the victory over those ancient enemies of sin and death. He has shown once and for all that this is God's world, and God is in charge here. And all those things which are incarnate in Jesus' life—love, truth, righteousness— are shown to be, not only beautiful, but also powerful. They are going to win. Okay, we see all of that in the resurrection. Now, the question is: what are we going to do about it? How will we respond to it? As Mark tells the story, it is unfinished. It is left for us to finish the story by what we say and by what we do. Can people see something of Christ in us? Can they tell, by looking at our lives, that something has happened to make us qualitatively different? Can they tell that Christ has happened to us? Tell me, what is the gospel according to us?

Perhaps we can get a clue about what we should do by looking at what the disciples did in the other gospel accounts. They responded to two invitations: First, come and see. Then, go and tell.

Look first at the story in the gospel of Matthew. In that account, Mary Magdalene and the other Mary went to the tomb early in the morning on Sunday. They were not expecting a resurrection any more than any of Jesus' other followers. They went to the tomb to finish wrapping the body of Jesus with spices, a job they didn't have time to finish on Friday because the Sabbath was about to begin. They found that the stone sealing the tomb had been rolled away. The tomb was empty. And an angel announced, "I know that you are looking for Jesus who was crucified. He is not here; for he has been raised, as he said. Come, see the place where he lay. Then, go quickly and tell his disciples."

They went running from the tomb, their pulse racing, their joy mounting. And while they were running, Jesus met them. And the first thing he said was, "Don't be afraid!" What good news that is! Often you have heard me say that in the Bible, the opposite of faith is not unbelief. The opposite of faith is fear. That's why, again and again we are told in scripture: "Fear not...Let not your hearts be troubled....Don't be anxious...Don't be afraid." The basic choice we have to make in life is: shall we live by fear or by faith? Because of the resurrection, Jesus says that we don't have to be afraid, we don't have to be afraid of anything.

God is. God is like Jesus. He is loving and powerful. He is in charge and He is going to win. We are in His loving and powerful hands. So, we don't have to be afraid—ever!

The two Marys were invited to "come and see." Once they saw, they went running to tell the story. Running. Running. There is an urgency about the gospel. There is an excitement about it. You don't linger. You don't stroll. You run to tell the good news of resurrection.

In the gospel of John, Mary Magdalene told Peter and the disciple Jesus loved that the tomb was empty. When they heard it, they, too, started running. They raced each other even. There is that urgency again. Running. They, too, were invited to "come and see." That was a recurring theme in Jesus' ministry. Whenever anyone questioned what he was doing or why he was doing it, he would always invite them to "come and see." Jesus insisted, "By their fruits you will know them," so, "come and see."

That's Jesus' invitation to us as well. Do you believe that Jesus has been raised from the dead? Do you believe that Christ is with us now, as the risen and living and indwelling Lord? Do you believe that by living your life by faith in him your life will be ever so much better? Well, come and see. Try it out.

How do we know the truth of resurrection? How do we know the truth of the gospel? Let's look at how those first followers of Jesus recognized the risen Christ and began to live again as faithful disciples. Thomas—you remember doubting Thomas. He said that he would not believe unless he could touch the nail prints in Jesus hands and feet. So, Jesus said, "Okay, have at it. Come and see." I like that. There is nothing to hide. Ask your questions. Probe with your inquiring mind. Look everywhere there is to look. The more truth you find, the more God you find. God has nothing to fear from honest questioning. If you are like Thomas, at the end of all your searching you may recognize who he is. And then, like Thomas, you may be able to say, "My Lord, and my God".

The two followers of Jesus on the road to Emmaus recognized the risen Lord in another way. They walked together, they talked together, they studied the scriptures together—but in all of that they did not recognize him. Finally they recognized him "in the breaking of the bread." They had shared many meals together. When he did that familiar thing, the breaking of the bread they said, "It is the Lord." That is a suggestion to us that we meet him and recognize him in worship, especially in the Lord's Supper. Jesus told us to break the bread and drink the wine "in remembrance of him." So, we affirm that when we do that, in faith, Christ himself is present with us, giving us his gifts of love and forgiveness and guidance and strength. "Were not our hearts burning within us," they said. That happens again and again as we come together in worship. I remember some of the first words we sang in youth choir as a Call to Worship: "Jesus stand among us, in thy risen power; let this time of worship be a hallowed hour." I experience that. I meet him here, recognize him here, in worship.

Of all the ways of recognizing the risen Christ, I especially like the way Mary Magdalene recognized him. She met Jesus, there outside the tomb. But she was weeping, thinking that someone had stolen Jesus' dead body, and she didn't know where to find him. Thinking him to be the gardener, she asked for his help. Jesus called her by name, "Mary." And that's when she recognized him. It was a very personal, intimate moment, when he called her by her name.

It is always so when we hear our name called. When our name is called, it means that we are recognized as a distinctive, unique individual. We are not lost in the crowd. We are known by our names. And the good news is that every one of us is known by name. And, when we are open to it by faith, the risen Christ makes himself known to us as he calls us by our name. Listen. Do you hear it? He is singling you out. He is calling your name.

Some of us are leaving for Israel tomorrow. Some others will be leaving in about 10 days. For us it is not just another tour. It is a spiritual pilgrimage. Like the first century disciples, we are running to the tomb. We expect to find that it is still empty. And what we hope for, more than anything else, is to experience there the risen and living Christ, who will place joy in our hearts and a song on our lips. Because that's what always happens when we meet and recognize the living Christ. That's what always happens when Easter becomes real.

Whatever you have to do to make that happen in your life, do it. Accept the invitation to "Come and see." Run to meet him. Because, once you do, you will never again be the same.

As I said, those first century disciples responded to two invitations. The first was, "Come and see." The second was, "Go and tell!" Well, if you do the first, you can't help doing the second. Once you encounter the living Christ, you can't keep still, you have to run. And you can't be quiet, you have to tell.

Remember the entry of Jesus into Jerusalem on that first Palm Sunday? The people were shouting and celebrating, waving palm fronds. The religious leaders, fearful that an unruly crowd would arouse the wrath of Rome, told Jesus to make his followers stop, to be quiet. Do you remember what Jesus said in response? He said, "I tell you, if these were silent, the stones would shout out!"

You can't keep the good news of Jesus bottled up. You just can't. If you have met the risen Lord and recognized him, if you understand what God has done for us through his life, death, and resurrection, there comes to us such a joy, such an excitement, such enthusiasm that we just have to go and tell. And, if you can keep from telling that story, then that is evidence that you have no story to tell!

I think about the Apostle Paul who met the risen and living Christ on the road to Damascus. It turned his life around and he proceeded to turn the world upside down. And, from that day on, even though he was rejected, beaten, ship-wrecked, imprisoned, and finally killed, his life was filled with joy. Even while imprisoned in Rome, not knowing whether he would live or die, still he exuded joy. Listen to what he wrote to the Philippians: "I have learned in whatever condition I am, to be content....Rejoice in the Lord always. And again I say, rejoice!" Once you have met the risen and living Christ, how can you keep from rejoicing and telling others? Come and see. Then go and tell.

There is a beautiful anthem that expresses it. I was privileged to sing for awhile with the Atlanta Sacred Chorale, under the inspired leadership of Dr. Eric Nelson. Dr. Nelson took a song by Robert Lowry and arranged it, and that anthem has become the unofficial theme song of the Chorale. The words are magnificent. Listen:

"My life flows on in endless song, above earth's lamentation;
I hear the sweet, though far off hymn that hails a new elation;
Through all the tumult and the strife I hear the music ringing,
It finds an echo in my soul, how can I keep from singing?
What, though my joys and comforts die? The Lord, my Savior liveth;
What, though the darkness gathers round! Songs in the night He giveth;
No storm can shake my inmost calm while to that refuge clinging;
Since Christ is Lord of heaven and earth, how can I keep from singing?
I lift mine eyes; the cloud grows thin; I see the blue above it;
And day by day this pathway smoothes since first I learned to love it;
The peace of Christ makes fresh my heart, a fountain ever springing;
All things are mine since I am His—how can I keep from singing?"

Isn't that great? If what the gospel says is true—and I believe with all my heart that it is—if what the gospel says is true, how can we keep from singing? Once we have come to see, we must go and tell. And we must do it with joy and with song.

Do you understand, then, why I say I like the short version of Mark's

Easter story? It is an unfinished gospel. But it is our privilege to complete the story by the way we live and by the way we die, singing joyfully all the while.

There is a benediction that says it, and I'll let this be the final word.

"He came singing love. He lived singing love. He died singing love. He rose in silence. If the song is to continue, we must do the singing."

Prayer: God, our Father, enable us this day to meet the risen Christ in the deep places of our lives. As we meet him there, take away our fear and replace it with faith. Complete the gospel story in our lives by the faithful way we live and die. And, in the presence of our risen and living Lord, help us joyfully to sing the resurrection song! In his name we pray. Amen.

16.
Nothing But Jesus Christ, and Him Crucified

I Corinthians 2:1-2

When I was a student at Millsaps College, the Chairman of the English Department was Dr. Milton Christian White. He had been there forever, it seemed, and I thought he was ancient. He must have been in his 60's! He was a volunteer tennis coach, so I spent a lot of time with him. He was somewhat crippled with arthritis so that he walked with a kind of shuffle. He was balding and brilliant. (I have always thought those two go together.) He knew everything there was to know about English literature. I have vivid memories of the day I was sitting in his class, waiting for him to arrive. He shuffled in the door, walked to the front, ran a hand across his bald head, and said, "O, I just know so much, I don't know what to tell you!"

The Apostle Paul could have said that. He, too, was brilliant. He grew up in the cosmopolitan city of Tarsus, rubbing shoulders with all kinds of people, representing cultures from around the world. He was a Roman citizen. He spoke Hebrew and Greek. He was a Jewish Pharisee, and he had studied under Gamaliel which meant that he had been exposed to the best in Jewish tradition, and he took it all very seriously. He knew a great deal! There was much that he could have told the people of Corinth, much indeed. But, he said, "I decided to know nothing among you except Jesus Christ, and him crucified."

Isn't that amazing? Of all the things he knew, of all the things he had experienced, of all the information he had amassed, everything else paled into insignificance when compared to the good news of Jesus' crucifixion and resurrection.

Paul reminds me of the poster I saw once, the poster that said, "The main thing in life is to make the main thing the main thing." Well, Paul agreed with that. And, for him, the main thing was the story of Jesus, especially Jesus' crucifixion and resurrection. For twenty centuries the Church has agreed with him. The crucifixion and resurrection is the heart of the matter. No doubt about it. When the four gospel writers told their story, they spent more time telling about that than about anything else. They wanted to make sure that we heard that story and that we got it straight. When the early Church preached, inevitably they told that story. It's always been true, the main thing about the Christian gospel has been what God was doing in and through Jesus in the crucifixion and the resurrection. That's the main thing.

When we talk about it, we can't separate crucifixion and resurrection. I always talk about the crucifixion/resurrection event. It's as if they are two parts of the same event, and therefore cannot be separated. If there had been no crucifixion, there would have been no need for a resurrection. And, if there had been no resurrection, we would never have heard about the crucifixion. So, the two are inseparable. But, let's talk about them one at a time.

I.

First, resurrection. Throughout the gospels there are events through which God announces who Jesus really is and places his stamp of approval on him. There was Jesus' baptism, when the Spirit descended as a dove and God spoke, saying, "This is my beloved son in whom I am well pleased." There was the transfiguration, when Peter, James, and John saw the glory of God and Jesus was lifted up. But, of all such events, the resurrection was the supreme act of authentication. For all those able to see with the eyes of faith, there was no longer any doubt. Jesus is God's son. He is the way, the truth, and the life. And, all the things we see at work in Jesus' life—love, truth, righteousness—all of those things are authenticated as well.

On Friday, the day of crucifixion, those things seemed so weak, so vulnerable. If Jesus had died and remained dead, Jesus and all that he stood for would have been repudiated and defeated by the other powers at work in the world. And, if we had even heard about him, which is doubtful, we would have said, "Well, it would be nice if such a life could work out. It is a beautiful dream. But it just won't work in our kind of world. Jesus tried it and you see where it got him. It got him dead!" That's what we would have thought if the story had ended on the Friday of crucifixion.

But that's not where the story ended. Jesus did not die and remain dead. On that first Easter morning, Jesus got up from death and walked back into life. And we see from that, that love and truth and righteousness—all those beautiful things we see in Jesus—those things are not weak and vulnerable as we thought on Friday. In reality, they are powerful, and they are going to win. You can nail them to a tree, you can wrap them in grave clothes, you can seal them in a tomb, but you can be sure they are going to rise again, because they are of God! Not only beautiful and noble, but also powerful! In the resurrection, it is as if we are reading the last chapter in the book. We know how things are going to turn out. And, what we see is that, no matter what today's newspapers headlines may say, the last word is never spoken until it is God's word. Because, finally, this is God's world and He will not be defeated here. In that eternal struggle of love and hate, of good and evil, of truth and falsehood, make no mistake about it, God will win! And all the faithful will win with Him, and then live forever in the joy of His presence. We see that in the resurrection.

For the disciples, the resurrection and the giving of the Spirit at Pentecost was where it all came together. For all the time they were together, Jesus had been teaching them, trying to help them understand. But, early on, they just didn't get it. Even at the crucifixion, they ran away in fear, afraid they would be next. They were hiding behind locked doors, shivering in the dark. No faith, no hope, no joy. Then God reached into history and turned the sorrow of the crucifixion into the joy of the resurrection, and the disciples were never again the same. They came out of their hiding places and with supreme courage and joy, again and again they told the story of resurrection.

There is no doubt that the resurrection is *the* pivotal event in history. It was the resurrection that made the disciples new men in Christ, men of depth, men of conviction and courage, and gave them the power to turn the world upside down! Wow!

II.

But, we can't talk meaningfully about the resurrection without talking about the crucifixion. Without the crucifixion, Easter celebrates a hollow victory. We can't experience the ultimate in joy at Easter unless we first experience the depth of sorrow in Jesus' death, and get in touch with the reality that it all could have ended on Friday.

It is by no accident that the cross is the symbol of our faith. Wrapped up in that symbol is the story of a God so powerful that He is able to take that instrument of shame, of suffering, of sorrow, of death, and with His powerful hands, turn it into a source of love and hope and joy.

All the pages of sacred scripture come together in dramatic focus there at the cross. There is nowhere else in all the Bible that we see the great heart of God so clearly revealed as there at the cross. Look at it. Let it take hold of you in the deep places of your life. There is something, isn't there, about that man on the cross?

For two thousand years we have been trying to express the meaning of it in words. We have been trying to grasp it with our minds and our hearts. There is this theory and that explanation of what exactly was happening there. But the full greatness of it has eluded us. There are no concepts large enough. There are no words expressive enough. We cannot fully understand it, nor adequately express it, but we have experienced the power of it, haven't we? Somehow God Himself meets us there at the cross, forgives us, and claims us as His own. And whenever we receive that experience in faith, and embrace it, we are never again the same. There is something, isn't there, about that man on the cross!

What I am about to say does not express all the meaning of the cross, but I want to share with you what has become increasingly important to me. I don't know why it took me so long to come to it, but what I think is at the heart of the cross's power came to me relatively late in my life. I have come to believe that the most redemptive power in the world is the power of suffering love, love that loves enough to suffer on behalf of the one who is loved. I believe that the willingness to suffer is the earnest money of love.

That kind of love is redemptive. It has the power to make us new. I have learned in my experience that punishment is not redemptive. Threat is not redemptive. Coercive arm twisting is not redemptive. You may change behavior by using those methods, but you do not change people from the inside out by them. You just don't. What is redemptive is the love that loves enough to suffer on behalf of the one who is loved. That can touch us in the deep places of life and make us new.

Do you want to know who really loves you? Don't just listen to words about love. It is easy to say, "I love you." And don't just look at loving actions, when those actions are easy, or convenient, or inexpensive. No, any love worthy of the name has got to be costly. And that's why I believe that the one who really loves you or me is the one who loves enough to be willing to suffer for us. That's real love. As the scriptures say, "Greater love has no one than this, than to lay down his life." Love that loves enough to suffer—that's what we see at the cross.

Now this is something new in the whole history of religion. Centuries before Jesus, we had heard about a powerful God, a righteous God, even a loving God. None of that was new—but, a vulnerable God? A God who loves enough to suffer? That's new. That's powerful. And that's redemptive! That's what we experience at the cross.

I like the way Fred Craddock expresses it. Dr. Craddock is one of the greatest preachers alive today. He wrote about redemptive love, and since I like the way he said it, I will give him the last word. He wrote: "Sometimes a child falls down and skins a knee or an elbow, then runs crying to his mother. The mother picks up the child and says—in what is the oldest story in the world—'Let me kiss it and make it well,' as if mother has magic saliva or something. She picks up the child, kisses the skinned place, holds the child in her lap, and all is well. Did her kiss make it well? No, no. It was that ten minutes in her lap. Just sit in the lap of love and see the mother crying. 'Mother, why are you crying? I'm the one who hurt my elbow.' 'Because you hurt,' the mother says, 'I hurt.' That does more for a child than all the bandages and all the medicine in the world, just sitting on the lap. What is the cross? Can I say it this way? It is to sit for a few minutes on the lap of God, who hurts because you hurt."

Do you understand? The most powerfully redemptive force in the world is that love that loves enough to suffer. That's what the cross is all about. It's an expression of that love which is always in the great heart of God. And that's the love at the center of our faith.

Paul said, "I have to preach that! Of all the things I know, that's the main thing. And so, I decided to know nothing among you except Jesus Christ, and him crucified."

The hymn writer said it like this:

"When I survey the wondrous cross on which the prince of glory died,
My richest gain I count but loss and pour contempt on all my pride.
Were the whole realm of nature mine, that were an offering far too small,
Love so amazing, so divine, demand my soul, my life, my all."

Prayer: Thank You, Father, for loving us enough to suffer with us and to suffer for us. Thank You for reaching out to us through Jesus to save us, to forgive us, and to make us new. Help us as we live our lives each day to make the main thing the main thing, and thus live as if we are the loved, forgiven, claimed, and blessed children of God. In the name of that man on the cross we pray. Amen.

17.
I Never Promised You A Rose Garden

John 16:32-33

I first heard the words of today's sermon title when I was a teenager. They came over the radio in a country and western song. The words: "I beg your pardon; I never promised you a rose garden."

I encountered those words again a few years ago when they appeared as the unofficial slogan of the emerging nation of Israel. When Jews migrated to Israel and were asked to settle in "kibbutzim" in parched desert frontiers, they were reminded of the arduous task ahead by the signs posted all around the settlements. The signs read: "We never promised you a rose garden."

More recently I have seen the words again as the title of a book and a movie made from it. The book, a novel by Hannah Green, is about a girl who struggles with the help of a psychiatrist to emerge from an imaginary world and to enter the world of reality. But it's a real struggle. At one point, the girl throws a bitter remark at her doctor. She cries out: "What good is your reality when justice fails and dishonesty is glossed over and the ones who keep faith suffer?" The doctor responds quickly and just as emphatically: "Look here, Deborah, I never promised you a rose garden. I never promised you perfect justice. And I never promised you peace or happiness. My help is so that you can be free to fight for all of those things. The only reality I offer is a challenge, and being well is being free to accept it or not at whatever level you are capable. I never promised lies, and the rose garden world of perfection is a lie...and a bore too!"

I.

Perhaps that's a good place to begin today's sermon: "The rose garden world of perfection is a lie." The fact is, pain, struggle, difficulty—they are all normal parts of life. And everyone who lives very long in this world is going to experience his or her share of them all.

Every choice has consequences. Some choices bring good consequences. Other choices bring bad consequences. It depends upon the choice. So, sometimes we bring difficulties upon ourselves by the choices we make. On the other hand, sometimes our troubles are the results of choices made by others. And sometimes they just come, through no apparent choice—tornadoes, earthquakes, crib deaths, cancer—they just come, we don't know why. But we do know that difficulty is a normal part of life. And if we are not ready for that, we might as well sign off, because the difficulties are here!

Of course, there are people who deny that. They say that pain, difficulty, and struggle are all in the mind. If you pretend they aren't there, they will go away. Just think positively. Put on rose colored glasses and everything will begin to look and feel like a rose garden.

I know people who try to live on that basis. For them everything always seems to be so upbeat, positive, and happy that I sometimes wonder if they are living in the same world I am living in. In some respects I would like for my world to be like theirs, but not if it means that I must close my eyes to reality and live my life in a dream world that does not exist.

There is a sense in which that to accept difficulty as a normal part of life is to be prepared for it and to be strengthened for it. The worst position of all is to be surprised. I feel sorry for those people who have never learned to accept struggle as a normal part of life. They are utterly unprepared for what lies ahead. They take their Pollyanna philosophy and look out at life through their rose colored glasses and everything is great, just great, until someone they trust disappoints them, until one they love rejects them, until, in spite of their best efforts, they fail, until their health breaks, or someone close to them dies, or until the world explodes into war. When such things happen they are shattered. They are utterly unprepared. They never knew life could be like that!

Usually, when such things happen to us, our first reaction is to ask, "Why me?" But, don't you see, such a question comes out of a rose garden picture of life. A better question is, "Why not me?," because the experience of difficulty in life is normal!

One of the things that impress me about Jesus is that he is a realist about life. In talking with his disciples, he said, honestly, "In the world you have tribulation." That's the way it is. He never promised them and he never promised us a rose garden. He never promised that life would be easy or that it would be painless. In fact, almost from the day they began to follow Jesus, the disciples were in trouble. Much of the New Testament was written from prison cells. Few, if any, of the disciples died natural deaths. No, Christian discipleship did not involve a rose garden. That was not the promise!

That word Jesus used, "tribulation," is borrowed from the farm. When a farmer threshed his wheat, he used a "tribulum," a stick and a rope which he used to beat down upon the stalk to separate the wheat from the chaff. That's a dramatic image isn't it? It's as if Jesus is saying, "Often in life, you and I are going to take a beating." And there are no exemptions from that, not even for us Christians. Pain, difficulty, and struggle—those are normal experiences and they come to us all. We were never promised a rose garden, a painless, easy, totally successful and utterly enjoyable life. No, that's not the promise. And, anyone who promises you that is what the Bible calls "a false prophet." That's not the promise.

Jesus said, "In the world you have tribulation." We might as well accept it. We might as well expect it. That's the way it is. But that's not all Jesus said. Over against the tribulation, the beating we will take, over against that, there is a promise. He said, "But be of good courage. I have overcome the world." In other words, the promise is not that we will be spared the struggle, but that by his grace we will be equal to the struggle!

At the cross, Jesus faced the worst that life can do: betrayed by a friend, abandoned by his followers, put through a mock trial on trumped up charges, ridiculed, tortured, beaten, and then killed. The power of evil in this world nailed Jesus to the cross and left him there to die. He knew about life's tribulations all right. But the power of evil did not have the final word—he did! On that first Easter he rose from the grave and conquered those evil powers. And because he did, we can too. We need not be subject to them. "Be of good courage," Jesus said. "I have overcome the world."

We are not promised a rose garden. But Jesus promises us that in whatever wilderness we find ourselves, we will not be alone, but that he will be with us. And his grace and strength will be sufficient for us. The good news is that the same power that raised Jesus from the dead is at work in us. Therefore, we are equal to anything. We can cope with anything. We can overcome anything. God can even use our difficulties and bring something good out of them. All of that is possible because of God—God's grace and God's power.

I don't know about you, but my experience tells me that not only will I have to take some beatings in life, but also that, apart from God,

I will be beaten—utterly broken and defeated. Alone, I cannot stand up to life. That's why, for me, one of the most strengthening, encouraging verses in all of scripture is the one which assures us, "Remember, I am with you always, even to the end of the world."

I like the way Jesus talks to his disciples. He says, realistically but also compassionately, "In the world you have tribulation. But be of good courage, for I have overcome the world."

Do you remember what the psychiatrist said to Deborah in the novel I quoted at the beginning? He said, "The rose garden world of perfection is a lie." That's true. But it's okay. We can deal with it. Because there is God.

II.

The doctor also said one more thing which I would like to note. He said, "The rose garden world of perfection is a bore, too." Have you ever thought of it in those terms? Certainly I would not ask for a larger share of difficulty. I'd like to have far less than I have. But can you imagine a world without pain, without challenge, without struggle? Without such experiences life would be far different than it is now. And I would hazard the guess that without such experiences life would be far less than it is now. That's not a bad way to say it: life would be a bore.

It has taken me a great many years to learn that without struggle there is no growth, and without pain there is no depth. I still do not fully understand why the struggles and difficulties are an essential part of life. But I do know that once they occur, God can work with us to use them, to bring something good out of them. That is not to say that God causes difficulties so that He can use them. Not that. But once they come, for whatever reason, God can use them and even bring something good out of them.

There is no question that in my life the times of greatest anxiety, the times of greatest inner turmoil were also the times of greatest growth. When things are going well for me, I tend not to think new thoughts or try new patterns of living. I just put life on cruise control and drive on from day to day. That's called stagnation. But, when life confronts me with a question I can't answer, with a problem I can't solve, or with a situation with which I can't cope all by myself—such experiences push me into new ways of thinking and feeling and acting. And that's called growth!

I will never forget my beginning struggle to learn something about preaching. My professor was a well known, rather egotistical man, with a real gift for sarcasm. One of the students would begin a sermon in class, the professor would go to the window, throw it open, stick his head out, and shout, "My God, give me air!" One day I was reading to the class an Easter sermon I had written. I was attempting in my inexperienced way, to contrast people's preoccupation with fashion and the Easter bunny with the real reason for celebrating Easter. I had read no more than a few sentences when he interrupted me and exclaimed with his arms flailing, "Stop, McCormick, stop! If you introduce rabbits so early in the sermon, before you're through there will be rabbits everywhere!" And everyone laughed at me. That was painful. And, I'm convinced that that experience by itself was not helpful. When I went home, I had to have someone tell me that they still believed in me; that there was still hope that I could learn to preach. But that painful experience played a part, too. I was shamed into harder work than I had ever done before. I coped with the sarcasm, eliminated the rabbits, and made an "A" in the class! And I am convinced that that painful experience helped to make me who I am!

What I am talking about is profoundly true of all human relationships. If all there is to a relationship is fun and games, that relationship will always be shallow. It took me a long time to learn, but there is no such thing as a depth relationship without pain. If you have a close relationship, an intimate relationship, I am sure that that closeness has been formed as a result of some shared struggle. That's why army buddies, college room mates, members of athletic teams form such strong bonds—it's the shared struggle. I believe that just as it takes the cold winds and freezing temperatures of high mountains to produce the hardest timber, just as it takes a white hot furnace to produce the hardest steel, just as it takes struggle with doubt to produce the deepest faith, in the same way it takes going through some difficult experiences together to produce the deepest love relationships.

Patricia and I are approaching our 50th wedding anniversary, and I wouldn't go back to the honeymoon for anything. It's better now. Our love is deeper and stronger that it could possibly have been back then. And I am convinced that our relationship is good not in spite of our shared difficulties, but in large measure because of them. There were times when one of our children was ill and we took turns sitting up all night with them in a rocking chair. There were times when the money ran out before the month did, and we would go around collecting empty bottles to redeem, so we could buy some milk. There was the time when we wrestled with the decision to move twelve hundred miles away from our families to a place where we had never been and where we knew no one, in order to start our lives over again. And, of course, there have been the arguments, the misunderstandings, and the hurts—all normal parts of married life. But without all of that we could never share the love which is ours today.

The Arabs have a proverb: "All sunshine makes a Sahara." The psychiatrist said, "The rose garden world of perfection is a bore." Both are getting at the same reality. None of us would ask for more difficulty, but without it, life as we know it would be greatly diminished.

To add one more case in point: it is often said that no one can develop the sensitivity and feeling that a great artist must have unless he has known suffering. I read recently that Beethoven once said of Rossini that he had in him the makings of a great musician, if only he had had some failures and difficulties with which to struggle, but that his great gift was spoiled by his facility of composition. In other words, his music came too easily. He needed to be able to struggle. And so do we.

Struggles in life also can make us more caring about the difficulties of others. When we have been hurt, we can get close to others who have been hurt and be supportive of them. We know. We understand. We have been there. I love the quote: "In love's army, only the wounded soldiers can serve." I don't like the struggles of life. You don't like them either. But the fact is, without the struggle we become shallow spirits and weak and ineffective human beings!

Of course, difficulties in and of themselves do not produce positive results. We all know people who have allowed the painful experiences of life to make them bitter or so discouraged that they give up and stop trying. Everything depends upon what we do with the difficulties which are a normal part of life. The "Why me?" question isn't helpful. Resentment doesn't do us any good. Mere stoic acceptance is no better.

The best answer is the Christian answer. The Christian answer begins with God, with the kind of God we have come to know in Jesus. God loves us every one. God cares for us more than we care for ourselves. God doesn't intend for bad things to happen to us. Like any good parent, God wants us to have the very best that life has to offer. But He doesn't promise us a rose garden. He doesn't promise even us Christians an exemption from the normal difficulties of life. What He does promise is to be with us. He does promise that His grace and strength are sufficient for us. He promises to take the circumstances of our lives and work with them to bring something good out of them. He promises to win the final victory and that we will share in that victory!

I tell you, you can't defeat someone who believes that, someone who trusts in that! Listen! God is for us! And He is in the business of bringing good out of evil. There is absolutely no difficulty in life that God cannot overcome and use for good. Thinking of Easter as the pivotal event in human history, I like to say it like this: "Our God is in the business of bringing resurrections out of all the crucifying experiences of life!" And that is good news!

Schiller, a German author, had a story he loved to tell the children, and I want to close the sermon by telling it to you. Once upon a time, in the development of life, he said, the birds had no wings. They crawled around in the grass like squirrels and mice and other earth-bound creatures. They had no wings, no commerce with the sky. Then one day the Lord threw wings at their feet and commanded them to pick them up and carry them. At first it seemed very hard. The little birds didn't want to do it—those heavy, unwieldy things. But they loved the Lord, and in obedience, they picked up the heavy things and carried them on their backs. And do you know what happened? Over time, the wings fastened there, became attached to their bodies. Finally, the little birds caught on to it, that what they had once thought would be a hampering weight became the means by which they were released into the freedom of the sky.

Do you hear it? That's the way it is with so many of the struggles of life. We face our difficulty squarely. By the grace of God we cope with it as best we can. And then, so often, we discover that that very difficulty has introduced us to a new dimension of life, and has become the means by which we begin to fly!

Will you hear it one more time? Jesus never promised us a rose garden. He said, "In the world you have tribulation. (That's the way it is.) But be of good courage. I have overcome the world!" And we can too!

Prayer: Father, we still don't know why life is as frustrating, as painful, as difficult as it is. In all honesty, we must say that we wish it were easier. But we are grateful, Father, that You have not left us alone to live only by our own resources. We are grateful that You are with us, and that You are always working to make life good for us. Help us to know that so many of the experiences we call burdens You intend to be wings. Help us to carry them gracefully, Father, and by so doing, help us to fly. In the Master's name we pray. Amen.

18.
What Is That In Your Hand?

Exodus 4:1-5, 10-17

The dominant figure of the Old Testament is Moses. He stands head and shoulders above all others in the history of Israel. He is Moses, the deliverer, the one who led the Hebrew people out of Egyptian captivity. He is Moses, the law-giver, the one who came down from Mount Sinai with the tablets of the law. He called the people into covenant with God, and led them through the wilderness to the land of promise. There is no doubt about it: Moses towers above all others in the Old Testament!

And yet, when we first meet Moses in the opening chapters of Exodus, he seems remarkably human. In fact, he looks and sounds a great deal like us.

I.

There he was, minding his own business, tending the sheep of his father-in-law, when God appeared to him out of a burning bush. God said, "Take off your shoes, for the ground on which you are standing is holy ground." An ordinary place, Moses thought. But every ordinary place becomes extraordinary indeed when God is there. In that experience God called Moses to an admittedly difficult task. He was to go to Pharaoh, the most powerful man in the world, and ask that he release the Hebrew people from slavery.

We will never comprehend the enormity of that task unless we see the big picture. The Hebrews had been slaves in Egypt for hundreds of years. They were doing all the hard work, while the Egyptians lived in comparative ease and luxury. The Hebrews were slaves—no minimum wage, no OSHA, no Fair Employment Practices Commission, no labor union. The Egyptians could do with the Hebrews as they pleased, so things were pretty good for the Egyptians. And Moses was asked to go to Pharaoh and ask him to give it all up, to let the Hebrew slaves go. The only reason Moses could give for that was that God had commanded it. Most rational people can anticipate Pharaoh's response: "No way, Yahweh!"

What would you do if you had been in Moses place? Probably we would do just as Moses did. Most of us would not just say, honestly, "I'm frightened. I don't want to do it!" Instead, just like Moses, we would begin to make excuses and recommend some more qualified person. My, how humble we can be when we don't want to do something! Years ago, I heard a quote which I have not forgotten: "The person who wants to do something finds a way; the other kind finds an excuse."

Listen to Moses' excuses and see if they have a familiar ring. First, he said, "Who am I that I should go to Pharaoh? I'm just a sheep herder, and they are not even my sheep. I'm a nobody. Why should the most powerful man in the world listen to me?" And, you know, he was right. Everything he said was right. But God cut through all the excuses and said, "It doesn't matter who you are. I'll be with you." It was God's presence with him, God's willingness to work through him that made Moses somebody! Don't forget that.

Still, Moses persisted in his excuses. He said, "But, Lord, I am not eloquent. I am slow of speech and of tongue." If we were saying it, probably we would say, "Lord, I can't get up in front of people. Public speaking is not my thing!" But listen to what God said, "Moses, Moses, who made your mouth anyway. Do you think you can tell me anything about your mouth that I don't already know? Listen, you do what I ask and I will be with your mouth and teach you what to say."

Still, Moses persisted. He said, "Lord, please send some other person! There are others more qualified!" God refused to shift the responsibility, but He did give Moses some help. God said, "I know that Aaron, your brother speaks well. He shall speak for you to the people."

Now we're getting to the part of the story which really excites my imagination. With one last effort, Moses said, "Lord, it won't work. The people will not believe me or listen to me. They will say, 'the Lord did not appear to you.'" And God said, "What is that in your hand?" Moses said, "A rod." God said, "Throw it on the ground." Moses threw it on the ground and it became a snake and Moses recoiled from it. Then God said to Moses, "Put out your hand and take it by the tail." He did, and it became a rod again.

Look carefully at that rod, because throughout the story of Moses, that rod was the symbol of God's presence and power. It was the rod that struck the rock and produced water. It was the rod held up before the people, producing victory in battle. It was the rod held aloft and parting the waters of the sea. The rod of Moses—a powerful reminder of God's presence and power.

Here is the point: God took what Moses had, blessed it, and used it to accomplish His purposes. It was only a piece of wood, but Moses was frightened by the power of it when God took hold of it and used it. Only an ordinary rod, but when God touched it, it became extraordinary indeed!

II.

This story of Moses reminds us all that everyone has something which God can use for good. Everyone! It may be a talent. It may be experience or contacts. It may be money or other resources. It may be simply a praying heart and a loving spirit. But, whatever it is, often the most ordinary and most easily overlooked resources turn out to be the most valuable when touched by God.

I become discouraged, and I know God does, when we continue to use Moses' excuses. "Who am I? I don't have any talent. My gifts, my resources are too small. In the face of such large problems, what can one person do? Besides, other people can do it far better than I can!" Sound familiar?

We sometimes ease our guilt by thinking and talking about what great things we would do if we had greater talent or resources. But that's not the point, is it? The point is not what you would do if you had this or that. The point is, are you going to be faithful with that which you do have? That's the point! I remember a poem about it:

> "It's not what you'd do with a million, if riches should be your lot,
> But what are you doing today with the dollar and a quarter you've got?"

That's the point. I'm sure that God looks at every one of us, just as he looked at Moses, and asks us that same searching, penetrating question: "What is that in your hand?" It is something, you know. You have something that God can use. And success or failure in life is determined by the extent to which we allow God to use what he has entrusted to us.

Have you ever thought how insulting it is to God to assume that we have nothing worth contributing, or that what we have to give will make no difference? I cannot believe that God would create anyone without the capacity to contribute. I believe deeply that you have something which God can use. It may be obvious. It may be hidden. But if you are willing for God to use what you have, you may be surprised at what God can do with it. The important thing is to give what you have and to do what you can. Whatever it is, in God's hands, it will be enough.

There is a delightful fable from the Middle Ages that speaks to me. A tiny sparrow was lying on its back in the middle of the road, its little legs pointing up toward the heavens. A horseman came riding by, saw the sparrow, pulled his horse to a stop, and dismounted. He asked, "Why are you lying in the road like that?" "I heard the sky was going to fall today," the sparrow answered. The horseman laughed out loud and said, "Oh? And do you expect to be able to support the sky on those spindly little legs of yours?" The sparrow shrugged his shoulders and said, "One does what one can!"

Well, that says it, doesn't it? All we are responsible for in life is to do what we can with what we have to work with. That's all. We are not responsible for the gifts entrusted to others. And, we are not responsible for the outcome. That's God's business. All we are responsible for is doing the best we can with what we have. And the remarkable thing is that, once God has added His touch to our efforts, our efforts are enough.

I can't tell you how important it is to understand that the result is not our responsibility, the effort is. As someone said, the point is not our ability, the point is our availability! Once we begin to calculate our chances for success in the big enterprises of life, we will feel like giving up before we begin. Listen: our resources are always inadequate! God's people are always outnumbered, overwhelmed, and under-financed. History is full of causes that should have been lost causes if we looked only at the obvious. But, again and again remarkable, life-giving things have happened because ordinary people with limited resources were willing to give what they had to God. And in God's hands, those gifts were enough.

Realistically speaking, what chance did Moses have, going up against the vast power of Pharaoh with only a stick in his hand? But that stick was more than an ordinary stick because it had been touched by God. Moses succeeded in leading the Hebrew people out of slavery toward their promised land. He gave what he had to God, and it was enough.

I think about that delightful story of David going out to do battle with Goliath. Remember, he first tried to put on Saul's armor. But it was too big and it didn't fit. In fact, it weighted him down so much that he was immobilized. That's what happens when we try to act like someone else. How silly we look trying to be something we aren't. But God came to David and said, "What is that in your hand?" David said, "A slingshot, a slingshot and a few pebbles." Most people would look at that scene and say, "But Goliath is wearing armor. He has a sword and shield so big that

David couldn't even pick them up. And, he's huge! What chance does David have against such a man?" But God said, "A slingshot, eh? Well, it's not much, but it's you. And it'll do!"

Do you remember the time Jesus was up on the hillside, teaching. There were 5,000 people there, and they became hungry. Jesus approached a little boy and said, "What is that in your hand?" The lad said, "I have five loaves and two fish." But, 5,000 people! How can you feed so many people with such a small lunch? But, Jesus said, "Five loaves and two fish. Well, it's not much, but it'll do."

There was Rosa Parks. She was the black woman in Montgomery, Alabama, who got on a bus one day and was so tired she just sat down in the first available seat rather than going to the back of the bus. That seemingly insignificant incident launched a bus boycott in Montgomery and thrust an unknown local pastor named Martin Luther King, Jr. to the forefront of a civil rights revolution. God asked Rosa Parks, "What is that in your hand?" She said, "A bus token." A bus token! What kind of weapon is that to throw against centuries of injustice and deeply entrenched tradition? But God said, "A bus token, eh? Well, it's not much, but it'll do."

Look at the Disciples. A collection of nobodies. They weren't wealthy or powerful or influential or well educated. How can you start a world wide movement beginning with people like that? God looked at them and said, "Well, they're not much. But they'll do." And they turned the world upside down!

III.

As I read the Moses story, the most significant part of all is the promise made by God: "I will be with you. You are on a divine mission, and I will never leave you." It is God's presence and power that makes all the difference!

Giving what they had to God, inadequate though it always is from a human point of view, many people have started organizations and institutions to help others. Laura Moore, Jack and Glenda Mitchell, Jacque Jacobs, and John Feicht are just a few whose names we know. I am sure that each of these would be the first to say that their dreams would have been impossible if they had been left to their own resources. But, when you give what you have to God and He begins to work with it, what we give is always enough.

There is no other way to understand history, and certainly no other way to understand the Bible. Again and again, from all outward appearances, good causes should have been lost causes. But so often the unlikely thing has happened because the hand of God was at work in it. A Moses persuades a Pharaoh, a multitude is fed by a box lunch, the mighty Roman Empire is toppled by a little band of faithful nobodies, and a dark and gloomy Friday gives way to a glorious Easter, all because of God.

That has happened so often in history that we should have gotten the idea by now. Success in any venture is not dependent upon our talent, our cleverness, our goodness, our hard work. No, success, finally, is dependent upon the power of God at work in our lives, and nothing else, nothing else! We have to be willing to give what we have. But the reassuring promise of God is, "I will be with you!" Never underestimate the power of that presence!

I leave you today with the question God asked Moses: "What is that in your hand? What do you have that God can use?" It may not seem to be very much. But, whatever it is, give it to God. In His hands, it'll do.

Prayer: Loving Father, we know now that each of us has something You can use for good in Your world. Help us to know that the gifts we hoard selfishly shrivel up and die, but the gifts we give to You are enlarged and used for the good of all Your children. Every moment of every day, assure us that You will be with us, that Your power and strength will be at work in us, making whatever we have to offer, quite good enough. In Jesus' name we pray. Amen.

19.
Being Christian in the Family

Matthew 7:24-27

When the Empire State building was being planned, there were cynics who said that you can't build a building out of concrete and steel 102 stories high. It is impossible. The whole thing will come crashing down! However, engineers said that there is virtually no limit to how high you can build, providing the foundation is deep enough and strong enough.

Jesus was a builder. He understood the importance of foundations. That is why he painted the vivid picture contrasting sand and rock as foundation materials. Obviously, the point is that some materials make better foundations than others. Jesus was saying that if you want to build durably, you had better build on Christian foundations.

This word of Jesus is relevant for us as we think about the family, because the family has foundations too. The family is strong or weak, and the individuals in the family either helped or hurt, depending upon the foundations on which the family is built. I believe that there is no other influence in the world which can even begin to compare with the family in molding individuals and in shaping society. So, we had better be careful about the foundations on which we build our families—so much is at stake. That's why I want to talk with you about "Being Christian in the Family." Listen carefully as we listen to Jesus about foundation material!

I.

First, in a Christian family, every person will be surrounded with durable, dependable love. To be loved like that may be the most basic of all human needs. Jesus knew of our need for it; that is why he said, "Love one another, as I have loved you." That is the way the Christian gospel works. We receive love from God and then we pass it on to one another. We cannot give that which we do not have, so we must first receive love from God, then we have something we can share. That is basic to Christian theology.

Almost everyone agrees that love is the basic human need. That is why it is so shocking to realize that so few people feel really loved. It is almost as if we assume that because we acknowledge people's need for love, somehow that acknowledgement meets the need. It doesn't! I know so many people who take great care to see to it that their families are well fed, well clothed, well housed, well educated, and well entertained. But they are not equally diligent in insuring that their families feel well loved. Yet, nothing is more important!

When I talk about the kind of love that looks and sounds like Jesus, I mean love without strings, love without conditions attached. So many times we say, "I love you." But what people hear is, "I will love you if...I will love you when...I will love you as long as..." Do you hear the conditions? So many people think of love as a reward to be earned, something to be deserved. They don't really believe that they will be loved no matter what!

Yet, that is the basic emotional need of the human race. We all need to feel that there is somewhere we will be accepted just as we are, somewhere we will still be cared about if we mess up, somewhere where we are special, where we are valued, not because of anything we have done to deserve that, but just because we are! It is a love we can depend upon, a love we know will always be there, a durable, dependable love. And the best place to get that is at home.

During our children's growing up years, we always tried to express our love, support, and pride when they made good grades, when they played or sang in a concert, when they received an award, or when they were models of good behavior. That is important. But at such times I wondered if they thought they were receiving love because they deserved it. That worried me, because the corollary of that is that if they receive love only when they deserve it, then when they don't deserve it, they won't receive it. That is why we took special care to express love for our children when they didn't deserve it, because such occasions gave us a rare opportunity to demonstrate the dependability of our love. We welcomed such opportunities. If they were loved when they didn't deserve it, then they knew it was a love without strings. It was dependable!

Is there some place in this world where you know that you are valued and cared about no matter what? Is there some place where you are loved with a durable, dependable love? If so, you are so very blessed. That comes close to being our deepest need.

Some time ago, there was an article in the Los Angeles Times about Howard Maxwell and his four year old daughter, Melinda. As children often do, Melinda developed a fixation on the story of "The Three Little Pigs." Every time her father came around, Melinda wanted him to read it to her. Well, for adults, a little "Three Little Pigs" goes a long way. The father, being both modern and inventive, got a tape recorder, recorded the story, and taught Melinda how to turn it on. He thought that had solved his problem. But it lasted less than a day. Soon Melinda came to her father, holding out "The Three Little Pigs" and asking him to read. Somewhat impatiently, the father said, "Melinda, you have the tape recorder, and you know how to turn it on!" The little girl looked up at her father with her big eyes and said, plaintively, "Yes, daddy, but I can't sit on its lap!" Of course, what she really wanted was love. That is what we all want, and we never outgrow our need for it. To be valued, to be cared about, to be loved with a love without strings, a love that will always be there for us; I tell you, that is a foundation for our families that is strong enough to build upon!

II.

The second foundation I want to talk about is family values strong enough to build upon. It is sad the extent to which most of us have been seduced by material values. When we think about the needs of our families, we tend to think first of material needs. Of course, it is good to have money and the things money can buy. But it is a good idea to check periodically to make sure that we also have those things that money cannot buy.

I will never forget an image which burned its way into my mind. It was at the beach. A family had gone out together for an outing. They had placed their beach towels, their umbrella, and other assorted paraphernalia on the beach, then remembered that they had left something in the car. The father started back toward the car, leaving his footprints in the wet sand. Everyone on the beach watched as their kindergartener began to follow his dad, stretching his little legs as far as they would go to make his feet fit exactly into the footsteps of his father. Remember that scene, because that is happening in your family. Someone is setting some standards, and others are trying to live up to them, or down to them.

One of the best gifts you can give to your family is a set of solid, Christian values. It is a great thing when a person knows who he is, what he believes, and how he should act, and knows that he has the support of his family in all of that. How strengthening it is when a person is able to say, "Our family does this because we think it is important." Or, "Our family does not do that because it goes against our values." Harry Emerson Fosdick, one of the great preachers of a former generation said, "In the home where I grew up I was taught to obey something inside me, so that when I left home I took it with me." That is what I am talking about: solid values.

That kind of solid value structure does not happen by accident. It must be taught. So, let me give a special word to parents. Make time for your families. I don't know of many things that feel more like love than the gift of time. I grew up in a busy family. My father was a pastor and seemed always to be at a church meeting, or out visiting the membership. Often, when I played a tennis match, or participated in a concert or other school event, my parents were not there. Sometimes I wondered just how important I was. So, when Patricia and I became parents, we decided to do it differently. During our children's growing up years, when there was an open house at school, we were there. When there was a Little League game or a concert, we were there. We left no doubt about our children's priority status. And, as a result, today our adult children will tell you that they know that they are loved.

Also, parents, don't be wishy-washy about standards, about expectations of your children. At every age our children need to know where the fences are. They will test us and they must test us to know how far they can go. The fences must be moved out and more freedom given as they grow older and more able to handle freedom. But the fences must always be there. That is what gives children security. That is what assures them that mature adults are in charge of their world and they are safe and secure inside the fences. The fences assure them that they are loved, because we really do care about what they do.

An Arizona teen-ager taught me that lesson years ago. She came to my office one day in tears, crying as if her heart would break. Do you know what her problem was? She said, "My parents let me do anything I want to do." That meant to her that her parents didn't really love her— certainly not with a wise love—because if they loved her they would care about what she did. The fences would be there!

I am saddened by the number of wrong things happening in the world in the name of love. I see so many parents being overly permissive in the name of love. They say, "I love my children so much that I just give in to them." But that is not what is happening. We don't give in to our children in unhealthy ways because we love them; we give in because we want them to love us. And we are afraid that if we say "No," they won't love us. Don't you see, the truth is in the opposite direction from where we think it is: unless the fences are there, our children will feel that we do not love them.

Hear me loud and clear: strong, wise love is able to risk not being loved back. If Jesus had given people what they wanted, he would not have been crucified. But, he gave them not what they wanted, but what they needed, and they killed him for it. Strong, wise love does not always give what people want; it gives what they need. You do that and the time will come when your family will thank you for it. That is something strong enough to build upon: solid Christian values.

III.

One final thing. Of course, the cornerstone of a solid foundation for the family is Christian faith, affirmed and lived out. It is important for your family members to participate in worship and Sunday School together, to read the Bible together, to have prayer in your homes together, to make God a natural part of your conversation, and an important part of your family experience. Children should know beyond a shadow of a doubt that mom and dad love Christ and his church, and that is an important part of your lives.

Our children learn what is important to us. When I was a child, I was not free to decide whether or not to go to school, to do my homework, to brush my teeth, to take a bath, or to go to bed. My parents insisted upon such things, because they were important. And, doing them consistently helped to shape my life in important ways. My guess is that you are with me so far. You agree about the importance of such things. But, just as I was not free to decide about such things, neither was I free to decide whether or not to worship, to come to Sunday School, to participate in the youth group, because those experiences were also important to my parents. Don't you see, if you insist upon education and hygiene and nutrition and the like, but make church optional, you are speaking volumes about what you consider to be essential and what is disposable!

Our rationalizations are amazing. I hear people say with a straight face, "I don't come to worship because my parents made me go as a child." But I've never heard anyone say, "I don't take baths because my parents made me bathe as a child." Or, "I don't read books, because my parents made me read as a child." What nonsense. Thank God for parents who have high values and insist that their children take those values seriously. Thank God for parents who take Christ and his church seriously and seek to pass their devotion on to their families.

Of course, we must know that we teach more by our actions than by our words. I think about the father who insisted that his son go to worship and Sunday School each week. He talked often about the importance of the church and the life of faith. But, one day he was shocked into awareness when he heard his son ask his mother, "Mom, when will I be old enough to stay home from church like daddy does?" Daddy was teaching, wasn't he? And so are we. We teach not only at those moments when we intend to teach. No, for good or for ill, we teach every moment of every day, especially when we don't know we are teaching. We teach by the way we live our lives.

I take very seriously my responsibility as a parent and grandparent. I know that, every day, in so many ways, they are learning from me. Do you know what has been my greatest fear in life? I have feared that somehow I would be a stumbling block to my children and grandchildren. I have feared that when they come to Christ in faith it would not be because of me, but in spite of me!

What does your family see in you? Do you love Christ and his church? Does it show? Is there a consistency between what you say and what you do? If your child or grandchild is stretching out to walk in your footsteps, are they leading in the right direction?

I like what one little fellow said. It was in Sunday School. The teacher asked him, "How did you become a Christian?" He smiled, shrugged his shoulders, and said, "I don't know. I guess it just runs in our family!" There is no greater gift you can give to those you love than for them to be able to say, "Being Christian just runs in our family!"

Do you remember what I said in the beginning? "There is virtually no limit to how high you can go, as long as the foundation is deep enough and strong enough." Well, how about this for a foundation: durable, dependable love; strong Christian values; and Christian faith, affirmed and lived out. That is quite a foundation, one strong enough to last!

Prayer: Father, be with us in our families as we seek to love one another as You love us: wisely, strongly, dependably, and without strings. In the name of Jesus we pray. Amen.

20.
Two Worlds

Genesis 1:31, Matthew 5:13-16

I was a young pastor attending a seminar. The featured speaker opened his mouth to speak, and these were his first words: "You and I are living today in a world God did not make. He allowed it, but He did not make it." That took place many years ago, but I still remember those words vividly. And, I remember the surprise I felt upon hearing them. It had never occurred to me that there was anything God had not made. I now see very clearly that he was right: "You and I are living today in a world that God did not make. He allowed it, but He did not make it."

The creation story recorded in the book of Genesis describes a world of beauty and harmony—a world in which every part cooperated with God's intentions. Everything was exactly what God created it to be. God looked at that world He had made and said, "It is very good!"

Then God created us human beings and gave us the freedom to think and to act for ourselves. He placed us in charge, giving us dominion over this world He had made. And, when God gave us freedom, He wasn't kidding. We are really free, free to do whatever we choose, even to rebel and to go our own way. Of course, what God intended was for us to exercise our dominion over the world by doing things as He wanted them done. Our dominion over the world was intended to be exercised within the context of God's dominion over us. But, free we are. We are free not to do it His way. So, when we use our freedom unwisely, or even rebelliously, God allows His world to go in a direction He never intended. So, do you understand the truth that seminar speaker was getting at? "You and I are living today in a world God did not make. He allowed it, but He did not make it."

I.

What kind of world am I talking about?

First, it's a hungry, sick, and hurting world. Thousands of people die each day from starvation or disease. Many live their entire lives in illiteracy, never being able to read or write. Many others live on the ragged edges of life, barely hanging on, existing but not living. Still others live in oppressive circumstances, never knowing freedom or dignity or security, let alone able to enjoy the good things of life. I don't have to dwell on it; you have seen pictures on TV, and on the internet. And, as unpleasant as it is, those pictures are real—they are pictures of real people with real feelings and real needs, most of them children.

That tragedy is compounded by the fact that, we can grow enough food to feed the world. We have medicines that can heal many of the diseases. We know how to educate. The developed world knows how to do so much more than we are willing to do. But, clearly, it's a hurting world, and every sensitive person of faith must know that God never intended a world like that.

Second, it's a divided world. Instead of living together in harmony and mutual cooperation, our world is fragmented in so many ways: the haves from the have nots, race from race, clan from clan, religion from religion, political system from political system, economic system from economic system. I could go on and on, but you get the idea. It's a divided world.

And, that begets an angry world and a violent world. Instead of talking with one another and reasoning together to resolve our differences and solve our problems, we resort to shouting at one another, and finally to seeking to destroy one another. Angry congressmen shouting at one another, a driver caught in traffic, sitting on his horn, and finally a young man strapping explosives to himself and blowing himself up in order to take some enemies with him—and the rest of us living in fear as a result. A divided, angry, irrational world—not what God intends.

Finally, it's a confused and frightened world. Increasingly, people are wondering what we can believe in, what we can trust and where can we be secure? Where is there something solid we can take hold of in this kind of world? People want to minimize the hurt of life and maximize the living potential of life—people everywhere want that—but they are not at all sure how to do that. To too large an extent, it's a lost world. Many people have never heard the good news of Jesus. Many who have heard it, have heard a distorted version of it. And many have heard, but have rejected it, and so continue to live less than full lives. So many people feel that they are adrift alone in a small boat with no rudder out there in the midst of a dark and limitless and stormy ocean. The ocean is so large and threatening, and our boat is so small. It's a confused and frightened world—not at all what God intends.

That's the world we live in. Knowing that, I can understand what a medical doctor said to one of his stressed out patients. He said, "What you need is an extended vacation on another planet!"

Of course, that's not the whole picture. Thank God that's not the whole picture. There are still many good, positive, hopeful dimensions to our world. There are caring people, helpful people, altruistic people. There are organizations and movements acting heroically for the larger good. If there weren't, we'd have a hard time surviving. But, I'll bet you recognize the world I have described. The point is: much is not right with our world. The world we live in is not the world God made and not the world God intended. God created a good world with enough natural resources to provide for the needs of all His children. God gave us minds, which, if properly applied, could solve so many of the problems which plague us. God created a world in which He intended for people to live together as brothers and sisters, as children of the same Father. He intended for us to work together lovingly and helpfully, pooling our resources to provide for the needs of the whole human family.

It's clear, isn't it? There is an obvious and painful gap between the world as it is, and the world as God intended it to be. And, that gap explains most of the pain, most of the difficulty we see. It's true. "You and I are living today in a world God did not make. He allowed it, but He did not make it."

II.

The question is, what can we do about it? In our kind of world, it's easy to feel helpless, to feel that the world is running us instead of us running the world. It's easy to feel trapped, to feel like helpless victims of a world gone mad, a world we are powerless to change. I am only one. What can I do? You've felt it, haven't you, just as I have?

But we are not helpless, no matter how we may feel at a given moment. There are things we can do, things that will make a difference. I remember the man who went out to the beach. He saw the starfish washed up on the shore, lying there, dying. He walked along, picking up starfish and tossing them back into the water. A cynic came along and said with a sneer, "Do you know how many millions of starfish have been washed ashore all around the world? What difference can it make if you throw a few back into the ocean?" The man never hesitated for a second. Continuing his work, he would toss a starfish back and say, "It makes a difference to that one….It makes a difference to that one."

I like that. I am only one, but I am one. I can't do everything, but I can do something. What I can do to make a difference I ought to do. And I trust that God will use that somehow to help redeem His world.

We who are followers of Jesus must first get our own houses in order. We must take hold of the vision of the world God intends—a world in which God is our Father and we are all brothers and sisters, responsible for helping one another live the good life. Once we take hold of that vision, we must commit ourselves to help make it a reality, whatever the cost. For those of us committed to God's kind of world, the key question in every issue is, "What is it that God wants for His world?" And when we live above the standards of the present world, we help to change those standards.

Isn't that what the scripture from Matthew is about? Jesus says that our Christian influence works like salt in food, like leaven in a loaf of bread, like a candle in a dark house, like a city that is built on a hill. As we live lives that look and sound like Jesus, we are, bit by bit, helping to shape His world according to His purposes.

Remember, the Christian movement began with Jesus and twelve followers. Not a very large or impressive group was it? But they had a dream of the way life, the way the world should be, could be. By living above the prevailing standards, and by trusting God for the rest, they succeeded in turning the world upside down. We follow in their footsteps, and all the resources of God that were available to them are available to us as well.

That's why we talk so much about mission. We talk about, think about, pray about the world as it is, contrasted with the world as God intends it to be. First, we want to celebrate all that God is enabling us to do to be of help. And then we want to hear about what we can yet do to change that world out there, to make it more user friendly, a better place for all God's children. We want to commit ourselves anew to making God's world what He intends it to be.

When we come to the bottom line, we really have only two choices: either we can be a part of the problem, or we can take hold of God's vision and strength, and become a part of the answer.

I like the way John Steinbeck wrote about our choices in his play, "The Short Reign of Pippin IV." In the play, the King puts on a disguise and goes to the little French town of Gambais. As he nears the castle, he notices that a statue of Pan has been removed from its pedestal and thrown into the moat. He sees an old man struggling to pull it out of the moat.

Pippin asks him, "How did it get into the moat?" He replied, "O, someone pushed him in. They always do, sometimes two or three times a week." "But why?" the King asked. "Who knows?" said the old man.

"There's people that push things in the moat. Pretty hard work too. There's just people that push things into the moat."

During the conversation, the King asks him, "Are you the owner here?" "No", he said. "I live hereabouts." "Then why do you pull them out?" he asked. The old man looked puzzled and searched for an answer. "Why—I don't know. I guess there's people that pull things out—that's what they do. I guess that's how things get done."

Well, there you have it. There are people who push things in and people who pull things out—that's our choice. Either we can be a part of the problem, or, by God's grace, we can be a part of the answer. Which do you want to be?

As Christians, as followers of Jesus, surely we know what we must be, what we must do. Because God has touched our lives with grace, we are changed. We can never be the same again. We can never be content, complacent about the way the world is, ever again. By God's grace, we have been touched and changed into the kind of people who go about pulling things out of moats. Where there is hurt, we try to heal. Where there is need, we try to help. That's just the kind of people God's people are.

I confess to you that, as I look at the world we live in, and as I look at all that needs to be done, I feel overwhelmed, and more than a little frightened. But I take immeasurable comfort from the realization that I am not alone. We are not alone. God is with us. And God has not abdicated. He is at work in His world for good. So, we do what we can where we are—we can't do any more than that, nor should we do any less—we do what we can where we are and we leave the rest to God, knowing that when we have given our best, that's enough!

I can't think of anything more challenging and exciting than that. Think of it: to be co-workers with God in re-shaping His world. To be instruments in the hands of God, helping to make God's world what He intends it to be. Wow! What a privilege!

Let us say it one more time, and I'll close with this. It was during the early days of television. A workman was placing television transmitters at the very top of the Empire State building in New York City. Seeing him at work up there, so far off the ground, a reporter thought this would make a fascinating human interest story. So, when the workman had completed his task and had returned to the ground, the reporter approached him and asked, "Aren't you frightened to work under conditions like that that? Isn't it dangerous to work so high off the ground?" The workman replied, "Yessir, it is dangerous." Then he added, "But then, how many people can say that they have changed the skyline of a city like New York!"

God offers us the privilege of changing the skyline not of a city, but of the world. We can help make this world more healthy, more humane, more harmonious, and more blessed. God made a good world. Now He wants us to help Him make it good again. We can do that. By God's grace, we really can do that. If we can, surely we must.

Prayer: God, our Father, we are grateful for the good world you have made and entrusted to our care. We ask Your forgiveness for any part we have played in making it less than good. Give us a renewed vision of the world as You see it. Inspire us and empower us to shape that world out there according to Your will. We pray in confidence that You are always with us and that Your grace and strength are always sufficient. In Jesus' name we pray. Amen.

21.
It's My Life, Isn't It?

I Corinthians 6:19-20

It was in an Ann Landers column some time ago—a letter from a grief stricken mother. Her son had died at the age of 33, weighing 560 pounds. His parents had warned him about the dangers of obesity. But he always replied, "It's my life. I'll do what I want with it."

As I read that, I remembered reading about a wife and mother who became bored with her life. One day she left her husband and family to go to Las Vegas with a man who had left his wife. Her only words were, "It's my life. It's the only one I've got, and I'm going to live it as I please."

There was the man who had despaired of life's meaning. He committed suicide, leaving behind a note which said, "I know that many people will condemn me for what I am doing. But, after all, it's my life isn't it?"

A teenager went out every weekend, bought a couple of six packs of beer and drank until he lost consciousness. His friends became concerned about him and told him so. He told them to mind their own business, adding, "I'm not hurting anyone but myself. And, it's my life, isn't it?"

Well, what do you think? How do you respond to such statements? Is my life mine to do with whatever I please? Is your life yours to do with whatever you please? Is it no one's business but your own? What do you think about the assertion, "It's my life, isn't it?"

I.

Well, in one sense that is an accurate statement. Your life has been entrusted to you. My life has been entrusted to me. And we can do with our lives whatever we please. We can mess them up. We can waste them. Or we can make of them something useful and noble. We can do with our lives whatever we please. And no one has any power to stop us. We are free!

Do you know what a gift that is? And what a responsibility? God has created you to be a special, unique individual. In the entire world, there is no one else exactly like you. You have been created to become a person that no one else can be. God has something in mind for you, and only you can be the person God intends. God gave us certain talents, inclinations, temperaments, gifts, to enable us to become that one of a kind special person.

But, because God wants us to be persons and not puppets, He has set us free. God wants the relationships of life to be real—relationships between us and others, relationships between us and God. And the only way for relationships to be real is for them to be entered into freely. That's one of the things that really impresses me about God—He takes us so seriously that He has given us freedom. He allows us to do with our lives whatever we please. We can mess them up, or we can fulfill God's dream for us. But the choice is ours. We are free.

Other people can care what we do with our lives. God can care. God can call to us and reach out to us and plead with us. But no one has the power to compel us. We can do with our lives whatever we please. So, there is a sense in which those people I talked about in the beginning are right.

II.

But, having said that, I must hurry to say a second thing: we are free to do whatever we please with our lives, but we are not free to make them turn out the way we want. Whenever we use our freedom to make a decision and to take an action, there are always consequences. If we do it right, there are usually positive consequences. If we do it wrong, there are negative consequences. But, for every action, there are consequences.

From the beginning to the end, the Bible insists that we are living in a morally dependable world. Our choices are not a matter of indifference because something important is at stake when we are deciding how to live our lives. That's the way it is because that's the way God has created the world to be. Our decisions are important because we are important.

And I'm here to tell you that just any old way of living won't do! What you sow, you reap. When you jump off a three story building, you expect the law of gravity to take you to the ground. The moral law works just as dependably. The law of sowing and reaping works just as dependably. If you lie continually, don't expect to be trusted. If you are undependable, don't expect to be depended upon. If you fail to give your best efforts at work, don't expect to be promoted. If you refuse to study, don't expect to make good grades. If you don't care about other people, and if you are unwilling to put yourself out for them, don't expect to have people lining up to be your friends. If you neglect prayer and worship and the reading of scripture, don't expect to be growing ever closer to God. If you plant corn, you'll grow corn. If you plant beans, you'll grow beans. What you sow, you reap. You can count on it. It's a law.

There is much in life I don't know, but I do know this: You will never arrive at a right destination by traveling in a wrong direction. We are free to do what we please with our lives, but we are not free to manipulate the results so that a life lived poorly will turn out well. It won't happen!

What I'm talking about is one of life's most difficult lessons. It's a difficult lesson because morals are for other people, we think. Consequences are things that happen to other people, we think. There is something about every one of us that makes us think of ourselves as the exception to the rule. We know that, generally speaking, irresponsible behavior results in negative consequences—but not for me! The rules don't apply to me. I can get away with it!

Isn't it amazing how we let ourselves off the hook? I can't tell you how many times I have listened to people say through their tears, "I knew it was wrong, but I didn't think anything bad would happen to me." Too late they learned that the moral law is no respecter of persons. What we sow, we reap.

I remember the young doctor in one of Lloyd Douglas' novels. He was bright, gifted, at the outset, idealistic. But, over time, he cut a corner here, made a compromise with his values there, until the night came when he came face to face with himself as he had become, and he didn't like the sight. In a drunken stupor he cried out, "You thought you could get away with it. You thought you were getting away with it. But, by God, you weren't. You weren't!" It's true, every day we sit down to a banquet of consequences. And we don't always like the taste of them.

If I believe anything, I believe that God has designed this world to function in a certain way. If we cooperate with God's intentions, by and large life is good. But if we play fast and loose with God's intentions, we suffer the consequences of that, and we cause other people to suffer the consequences of that as well. There is a way that leads to life. It's God's way. We are free to take another way. But if we do, we'll miss it. We'll blow it. We'll mess it up—because God has designed all of life to function according to His way.

I imagine some of you are thinking, "My, that's narrow minded. Why won't a number of ways work? Why can't I do what I want with my life?" Well, you can. I'll keep saying that: you can. You are free. Just don't expect it to work out very well.

Several years ago, I spoke at a Junior College in Mississippi. I remember saying to them: You love your cars. I know you love your cars. But not just any old way of driving will do. If you want really to enjoy driving your car, you need to take seriously the way the designer and builder intends it to function. Understand how the designer has built the car and then cooperate with that. You may say: "Why can't I do it my way? Why can't I step on the brake when I want to go faster? Why can't I turn the steering wheel when I want to stop? Why can't I turn on the windshield wiper when I want to turn? Why can't I turn on the radio when I want to adjust the temperature? Why can't I do it like that?" Well, you can. No one's stopping you. You can do with your car whatever you please. But if you choose to use it like that, don't be surprised when it doesn't work very well. Because that's not the way it was designed to work.

That's so obvious, isn't it? So obvious that we need not even say it. To me it is just as obvious that, if we want life to be good for us, we had better try to understand how God has designed it to work, and simply cooperate with that. I have to tell you that the most important thing I have learned in my years of life is that this world is designed to function in a God-centered way. Any other way just won't work very well.

III.

One more thing. Our lives are ours. We can do with them as we please, experiencing the consequences of that, both positive and negative. But, if we are at all sensitive and responsible, we will know that there is a claim placed upon our lives by everyone who has ever loved us. And our best chance in life is to respond to that love as it calls forth the best from within us.

Our scripture talks about it: "You are not your own. You were bought with a price." Teachers, coaches, friends, family members pay the price with their love. And, supremely, Christ pays it with His ultimate love given to us at the cross. Think back over your life and I know you will agree that everything good in life is the result of someone's love. Speaking personally, by their love so many people have invited me into good experiences. By their love, they have forgiven me and set me free of guilt. By their love they have encouraged me, supported me, and believed in me. By their love they have called forth the best from within me.

If I know that, if I care at all about that, I cannot live my life just any old way. To do so would be to turn my back on that. To do so would be to say that their love doesn't matter. I can't do that. Every person who has ever loved me has placed a claim upon me. And, the more I know that, and the more I live my life under the influence of that, the more I am the better as a result of that.

At the outset that may feel restrictive, limiting. In fact, it is the source of our greatest freedom. Not that false freedom to do as we please, but that greatest freedom, the freedom to do what we ought, to be what we ought. Love sets us free to be the best we can be!

I was privileged to have an elementary school teacher, Mrs. Johnston, who believed in me so sincerely. Whenever I was tempted to be less than my best, I could see Mrs. Johnston in my mind. I didn't want to be less than she thought I was. Her affirming love placed a claim upon me and shaped my life for good.

There was my band director, Houston Jenks. He believed in me as few other people have. He gave me a chance to prove myself. And whenever I was tempted to slack off and be less than I knew I could be, I remembered Mr. Jenks, and tried harder.

Every time I have been tempted to cut corners in my preaching and come into the pulpit less prepared than I should be, I remember Elizabeth Orde, and Burdette and Helen Boileau, and Bill and Carolyn Fulton, and Danny McKenzie, and Andy Johnson, and so many others, including members of the Chapel, who have encouraged me and dared to believe that God was using my preaching. I remember their trust, and I know I cannot let them down by being less than my best.

And, of course, my parents, especially my mother. So often she took the time to tell me of her dreams for my life. She let me know how special she thinks I am. How can you receive a love like that and then live your life as if it doesn't exist? How can you be loved with a love like that and then turn your back upon it? My mother's love has placed a claim upon my life. When I acknowledge that claim and allow it to shape my life, I am the better for it. I know that.

Of course, when Paul was writing his letter to the Church at Corinth, when he said, "You are not your own, you were bought with a price," he was talking about God's love which comes to us through Christ. He was talking about that redemptive, saving love which places an ultimate claim upon us.

Just think about it. God—the designer and creator of everything—

the one who sustains all life and the one who provides for all our needs—that infinite, inexpressible, all-powerful God loves you so much that He had to find a way to get through to you. For years He sent prophets and priests and holy people to spread His word. But it wasn't enough. Finally, He sent His Son. Jesus took upon himself our weakness, our vulnerability. He was rejected, betrayed, falsely accused, unjustly condemned, tortured, ridiculed, and finally nailed to a cross and left there to die. All of that to get through to us, to let us know of the depth of His love. If that doesn't do it, I don't know what more God can do! What more can one give than his very life?

How can we turn our backs on a love like that? How can we live our lives indifferent to a love like that? Oh, we're free to do it. We can walk away from it and do our own thing if we're determined to. But just understand, when we reject that love and its claim upon us, we are turning our backs on our best selves. And we are letting that abundant life that Jesus talked about slip through some crack in our fingers.

"You are not your own"—not if you're sensitive, not if you're responsive—"You are not your own. You were bought with a price." Christ's great love has placed a claim upon us!

In Mississippi there lives a woman who is old and tired. Her life has been hard, given generously on behalf of her only daughter. Her husband left her before their child was born. The wife was not well educated. She had no work experience, not well equipped to do very much. So, she took in sewing to support herself and her little girl. She worked late into the night most evenings so that she would have time during the day to spend with her daughter. She tried to make up for the fact that she didn't have a daddy. She made all of her daughter's clothes by hand. They were not only as good as, they were better than anyone else's in school. She always had party dresses and spending money and all the rest. Her mother saw to it.

The daughter grew up and got into trouble. Her mother bailed her out. She was married and divorced and her mother came to her rescue. The mother lived all her life on the ragged edge of poverty, but she never turned down a call from her daughter. Today the mother is old and wrinkled and tired. But she works on. She has to. She was never able to save anything because her daughter always needed something.

I don't know, perhaps the mother gave too much. Maybe she was over indulgent. Maybe she tried too hard to compensate for the lack of a father. I don't know about any of that. But I know the day will never come when that daughter will have a right to say, "This is my life and I will do what I please with it." No, her mother's love has placed a claim upon her, and that love is her best hope in life.

Do you hear it? Every one who has ever loved you has placed a claim upon you. Especially, God's great love made known to us in Christ has placed a claim upon us. When we know that and live our lives in the strength of that, then it saves us, and we are never again the same.

"You are not your own. You were bought with a price." I thank God for that, because that is our best hope!

Prayer: Father, we acknowledge the many claims upon us. Our lives have been strengthened and enlarged and enriched by the love of so many. Thank You, Father. Especially do we thank You for Your great love made known to us in Christ. We don't deserve it, but we are so very grateful for it. Now, in the holiness of this moment, we relinquish all selfish claims to our lives. We give our lives to You so that You may give us life abundant. In the Master's name we pray. Amen.

22.
Promises To Keep

Hebrews 8:10

Do you know the name Tom Dooley? Not the folk song Tom Dooley, but Dr. Tom Dooley? You need to know his story, because Dr. Tom Dooley was a twentieth century saint. While serving in the Navy, he saw the physical suffering of the people of Southeast Asia—so much illness and suffering, so few doctors to deal with it. When his tour of duty was over, he resigned his commission and went to Indochina, now Laos, to serve as a medical missionary. There he poured out his life on behalf of the people. He saw patients in consultation. He prescribed. He did surgery. But not only that; he also recruited and trained doctors and nurses. And, he raised money and built hospitals. Tom Dooley was a Christian, a devout Catholic. He had been made compassionate by the compassion of Jesus. And, he felt that he had received a call from God -a call to minister to the needs of those suffering people. His Christian commitment was symbolized by a religious medal he wore always around his neck. On the back of that medal he had inscribed some words by Robert Frost:

"The woods are lovely, dark and deep, but I have promises to keep,
And miles to go before I sleep, and miles to go before I sleep."

Because of his Christian commitment, he had made some promises to God. His healing ministry was his way of keeping his promises. He had come to love the people of Laos. And because of his love for them, he had made promises both to God and to them. He worked at fever pitch, sometimes driving himself to near exhaustion. How would he make a dent in the need? So much to do—so little time and resources with which to do it.

In the midst of all of that, it was discovered that Tom Dooley had cancer. The doctors told him that if he returned to the United States, availed himself of the best medical care, and got plenty of rest, he could extend his life by some considerable degree. But, his work was not finished. His commitment was not complete. So, he decided to spend whatever time he had left continuing his work there in Laos. If anything, he worked even longer hours. He continued to see patients, train doctors and nurses, raise money, build hospitals. He worked and worked and worked, until one day he collapsed, and shortly thereafter, he died.

At the funeral service, the priest told the inspiring story of his life— a life that looked very much like Jesus' life of compassion. He told of how Tom Dooley had invested his life in the healing of the people of Laos. He told of the medal he had always worn around his neck, and he read the inscription:

"The woods are lovely, dark and deep, but I have promises to keep,
And miles to go before I sleep, and miles to go before I sleep."

Then the priest added, "And now you can sleep, Tom Dooley, because you have kept all your promises." It's a marvelous thing to make big promises in life. Such promises give stature, meaning, and direction to our lives. It's a marvelous thing to make big promises. But it's an even better thing, once we have made big promises, to keep them. In fact, I can't think of anything I would rather have said about me at the time of my death than, "Jim McCormick made some big promises in his life. And when he made big promises, he always kept them!"

In the Bible, the word for promise is "covenant." And you'll never understand the Bible unless you understand covenant because, from beginning to end, that's what the Bible is about. A covenant is an agreement, a kind of two party contract in which each party to the contract makes certain promises. The thirty nine books of what we call the "Old Testament" should really be called the "Old Covenant" because that's what they are about. They are about the God who called a group of people together by means of a covenant. That's what made them the people of Israel. And in that covenant God promised, "I will be your God. I will watch over you with steadfast, dependable love. And, I will provide for all your needs." On their part, the people promised, "We will be Your people. We will follow You faithfully. And we will keep all Your commandments." That was the covenant. And, for their entire history, the people of Israel interpreted all the events of their lives in light of that covenant.

The twenty seven books of what we call the "New Testament" should really be called the "New Covenant" because that's what they are about. In the new covenant, God sent Jesus into the world. He called a new group of people together, the new Israel, or the Church. And again, promises were made. God promised, "I will be your God. I will watch over you with steadfast, dependable love. And I will provide for all your needs." And the people promised, "We will be Your people. Through faith, we receive Jesus as our Savior and Lord. We will follow You faithfully. And we will keep all of Your commandments." That was the covenant. Those were the promises.

Read the Bible, read the history of the Church, look at your own experience, and you will discover that God has always kept His promises. Century after century He has been utterly faithful and utterly dependable! When God makes a promise, you can take it to the bank. In fact, the dependability of God is one of the great themes of the Bible. When God makes a promise, He always keeps it. But, the story of human beings is something else; we are not very dependable. We are an erratic bunch at best. We run hot and cold, on again, off again, sometimes faithful, sometimes not. That's pretty much Judeo-Christian history in a nutshell: God makes promises and keeps them; we make promises and break them. I'm not proud of that reality, but reality it is.

Most of the contracts I know anything about have the provision that if one party fails to live up to the terms of the contract, the contract is voided. And often there are severe penalties involved. You can't expect one party to keep his part of the agreement if the other party doesn't keep his. That isn't fair! But the remarkable good news of the gospel is that God keeps on keeping His promises whether we keep ours or not!

Isn't that amazing? In spite of our faithlessness, God is still faithful. One of the great scriptural texts declares: "God makes His sun to shine on the evil and on the good, and sends His rain on the just and on the unjust." God never forsakes us; He never abandons us; and He never gives up on us. He continues to love us and to provide for us even when we turn our backs on Him. That tells us something important about the nature of God, doesn't it? His faithfulness is not dependent upon our faithfulness. His love does not wait for us to love Him in return. His determination to keep His promises is not dependent upon our keeping ours! Amazing! Hear it loud and clear: when God makes a promise, He keeps it!

Now, if I were God, I wouldn't do it like that. I would make my love and the passing out of my blessings a bit more conditional. I would make it clear that there are rewards for faithfulness and that there is punishment for unfaithfulness. I mean, you scratch my back, I'll scratch yours. You show me that you deserve what I have to give. I tell you, I would run the world in such a way that people would shape up, or they would be sorry!

For example, if you are not faithful, do you think I would allow you to have an excellent job, a comfortable home, and a good family? Not on your life. Such blessings would be reserved for those who deserve them! You have to keep your part of the bargain! If you planted a garden and were not faithful, I would have it rain right up to your property line, and stop. Not a drop on your crop! There would be perpetual drought until you took your faith commitment seriously. And, if you cut church and went fishing on Sunday morning—nary a nibble, not on Sunday morning! And, Sunday morning golfers? I would have every ball find the rough, or a bunker, or the water. I would have you three putt or four putt every green. No birdies, no pars—not on Sunday morning! That's the way I would do it if I were in charge. There would be some changes made, and I would have people shaping up right and left! Aren't you glad I'm not God?

The Christian gospel is such good news that I can't fully comprehend it. In spite of our unloveliness, God insists upon loving us. In spite of our unworthiness, God keeps on blessing us. In spite of our failure to keep our promises, God keeps on keeping His. Remarkably, in spite of our undependability, God insists upon believing in us. He continues to invite us to make promises to Him. And, when we do, He keeps on believing that we will keep them. I have come to believe that the heart of the gospel is not that we believe in God. The heart of the gospel is that, in spite of our track record, God continues to believe in us. And He continues to provide for us as a loving Father knows how to do. I tell you, that's some kind of love. It's a faithful, dependable kind of love!

Now, I don't fully understand love like that. But I sense in my depths that God's kind of unconditional love is my best hope in life. I don't know about you, but I don't respond well to threat and punishment and coercion. Such actions are not redemptive; they don't have the power to change me on the inside. But when it finally gets through to me that God provides for me whether I deserve it or not, that God continues to love me even when I don't love Him back—when God's unconditional, steadfast love gets through to me, something begins to happen to me. The best Jim McCormick begins to be called forth. I don't want to continue to take advantage of God's love, continuing to receive and receive and receive without giving in return. His love for me makes me want to answer His love with some love of my own. God's dependability in keeping His promises to me makes me want to answer that with some dependability of my own. I know when I am at my best that my best hope in life is precisely the dependability of God's love—that love that keeps on loving no matter what!

Every one of us has made promises to God. If you are a Christian and a member of Christ's church, you have made some promises to God. At some time in your life, you stood at the altar of His church and you said, "I accept Christ as my Savior and Lord, and pledge my allegiance to His Kingdom. I will be loyal to His church and uphold it by my prayers, my presence, my gifts and my service." We said that. And, if we have kept that promise, it has given direction and meaning to our lives.

Today, I can't help thinking of those faithful Christians who came before us and who also made some important promises. Because they kept their promises, this Chapel was organized, buildings built, worship services held, classes taught, faith kept alive and passed on from generation to generation. We are able to worship here today because of the kept promises of those who came before us. We stand today on their shoulders. And God will do great things among us in this generation, just as God did great things in generations before us, if we will be faithful

Promises. Promises. We are told in scripture not to swear. We are told, "Don't swear by heaven or by earth or by any other oath. Just let your 'yes' be yes and your 'no' be no." (James 5:12) Do you understand what he was saying? He was saying don't be the kind of person who has to prop up your words, feeling that no one will believe you unless you flail your arms around and say, "I swear by all that's holy..." No, we are told, "Just say 'Yes' or 'No'." That's enough. In other words, be a person of such credibility, be a person of such integrity, that everyone who knows you will know that, if you say it, you will do it. If you make a promise, you will keep it.

In closing, let me tell you about someone like that. His name was Billy, and it was the first year he was old enough to play Little League baseball. For years he had gone with his parents and sat in the stands while his older brothers played. But this was his year! Ever since he could remember, he had been looking forward to it. He was going to play Little League baseball! For weeks, he had been breaking in his glove. You know how they do it: throw the ball into the glove to form the pocket, and then take it out; throw the ball in the glove and then take it out. He and his mother had been to the sporting goods store to buy baseball shoes. They had bought a baseball cap with the team insignia on it. And he and his parents had gone to the meeting to sign up and to meet the coach. Excitedly, he had said, "My name is Billy, and I'm going to play on your team this year! When is the first day of practice?" The coach smiled and said, "Monday, 4:30, the baseball field next to the school." "I'll be there!" Billy said. The next day he ran into the coach at the shopping mall. He called across the full width of the mall, "Hey coach! Monday, 4:30, I'll be there!" The days passed. Several more times Billy saw the coach and every time he would say the same thing. He saw the coach at church on Sunday and said, "Tomorrow, 4:30, I'll be there!"

Monday came. Billy could hardly contain himself. He could hardly wait. The clock moved so slowly. Minutes seemed like hours. About noon, the storm clouds began to roll in. Mid-afternoon, the bottom fell out and the rain began to pour. It rained and rained and rained some more. The coach's house was located across the street from the practice field. As he was walking through the front room, he looked out at the field, and it was about 4 inches deep in water. There was no way they could practice that day. But as he looked, he saw a little boy standing there at the pitcher's mound, throwing a ball into the glove, taking it out; throwing it into the glove, taking it out. Grumbling under his breath, the coach put on his boots, his raincoat, his hat, took his umbrella, and went sloshing across the field. As he got close, he saw that it was Billy. The new baseball shoes were under water. Water was running off his new cap and down his face. There was not a square inch of dry clothing anywhere on him. Impatiently the coach shouted, "Billy, you're drenched. You're going to catch your death of cold. What do you think you're doing?" With all the innocence of youth, Billy replied, "Coach, I said I'd be here."

"I accept Christ as my Savior and Lord and pledge my allegiance to his Kingdom. I will be loyal to his church, and uphold it by my prayers, my presence, my gifts, and my service." We said that! It's a marvelous thing to make big promises in life. It's an even better thing, once we have made big promises, to keep them!

Prayer: God, our Father, we are grateful that You love us so much that You keep Your promises. We are grateful that You trust us so much that You invite us to have a part in what You are doing in Your world. We have made our promises. Now give us the grace to keep them. In the name of Christ we pray. Amen.

23.
It Is Also Blessed To Receive

John 13:1-8, Acts 20:35

One of the most meaning filled stories in the New Testament is the account of the last supper. It was the Passover, and Jesus and his disciples gathered in an upper room to share in the meal. It was customary, and an expected act of hospitality, to have someone there to wash the feet of those who had come. But there was no servant present, and the disciples were busy jockeying for the preferred positions in the coming Kingdom. They all wanted to be pre-eminent in the Kingdom, so none was willing to lower himself to such a menial task. But it needed to be done, so Jesus himself took a basin and a towel and began to wash the feet of the disciples.

I imagine that they were embarrassed because Jesus was willing to do what none of them was willing to do. If they weren't embarrassed, they should have been. When Jesus got to Peter, Peter couldn't take it. He said, "Lord, you will never wash my feet!" Don't you know how difficult it must have been for Peter to accept this act of humility and service from one he considered to be so much greater than himself. I mean, this was Jesus, the Christ, kneeling down in the dirt to be a servant to the disciples. Peter resisted. But Jesus said, "If I do not wash your feet, then you will have no part of me."

Most of what we talk about in that event was the act of humble service that Jesus rendered. In fact, he asked them later, "Do you understand what I have done for you? I have given you an example. You should do to one another as I have done to you. This is how people will know that you are my disciples, if you have love for one another." With the basin and the towel, Jesus gave them and us an example of servant love. Later, at the cross, he gave us the gift of suffering love. And that's what we usually emphasize—these two loving events.

But there is another truth here which we must not miss. When Peter resisted Jesus' gift of servant love, Jesus said, "If I do not wash your feet, then you will have no part of me." Do you understand what Jesus was saying? He was saying that the willingness and the ability to receive is essential to relationship. If Peter refused to allow Jesus to give him something, they could have no meaningful relationship. Relationship requires giving and receiving.

In the scripture I read from Acts, Paul reports some words of Jesus that are not included anywhere in the gospels. We get these words only from Paul. He reported Jesus saying, "It is more blessed to give than to receive." I have heard that scripture quoted all my life. Almost always the emphasis is upon the importance of giving, and that indeed is the primary emphasis. But Jesus does not say that we are only to give and not receive. No. By implication, Jesus is saying, "However blessed it is to give, it is also blessed to receive." Have you ever thought about that? It is not either/or. It is both/and. Clearly, in the totality of life we are to receive as well as give.

I.

To begin with, it is obvious that we must be willing and able to receive because we need it. Much of the time we would like to maintain the illusion that we are quite self-sufficient. We have within ourselves everything we need to live a full, happy, and successful life. So, we don't need anyone or anything else. Much of the time we'd like to think that, wouldn't we? But, in our more honest moments we know that is an illusion. We do need to receive—from God, and from other people.

We need to receive because that's the way God made us. You have heard me say again and again that life is about relationships. When you boil it all down, life is either good or less than good depending upon the quality of our relationships. We are not to live in isolation, but in relationship. And we are not to be self-sufficient; we are to be inter-dependent. We receive and give. Others receive and give. And, in all the receiving and giving, the relationships grow and life becomes much more like what God intends. So, if we understand life, we understand it is a two way street. We do not receive all the time without giving; but neither do we give all the time without receiving. Life involves a two-fold motion: we receive and we give, we receive and we give.

And the fact is, we cannot give unless we have first received. Our lives are not vast reservoirs of inexhaustible gifts for others. No, our supply of love, of caring, of helpfulness, and of all of the other gifts is limited. And we will exhaust our supply unless we are constantly re-stocking.

The Bible reminds us that, "we love because he first loved us." What that scripture is saying is that whatever loving or giving we Christians are able to do, is the result of receiving from God. We simply pass on to others the gifts we receive from Him. And we can be sure that we will soon run out of good things to give, unless we continue to receive.

I helped to lead a retreat for a Sunday School class recently. I told them about Ross Whetstone, a former staff member of one of the General Boards of the United Methodist Church. Ross is a charismatic Christian—I mean by that that he has received the gift of glossolalia—he speaks in tongues. Some of his fellow charismatics often approach him and ask if he is "Spirit filled." That's their code word for being okay or not okay in their circles. If you are "Spirit filled" you are okay; if not, you are not okay. When they ask him, "Ross, are you Spirit filled?" he said he always replies, "Sometimes I am 'Spirit filled' and sometimes I am not. My problem is, I leak."

Well, so do I. Sometimes my supply of God's Spirit and His love run out because I am passing them on to others. Sometimes the supply runs out because I become careless and neglect replenishing the supply. But the fact is, I cannot pass on what I do not have. And unless I am constantly receiving from God, I cannot pass his gifts on to others. When we read about Jesus in the gospels, we learn that Jesus spent a great deal of time in prayer. Clearly, he could not do the remarkable things that he did—loving, serving, and giving—unless he opened himself to receive from God. If Jesus needed that, how much more do we need it?

Psychologists tell us that we are incapable of loving other people unless we have first been loved. Unless we have experienced it, we don't even know what it is. We have to receive it before we can pass it on. Years ago, I was invited to speak for a Chapel service at a Children's Home. Before the service, the Superintendent suggested that I not use the term, "Father" with reference to God. Many of the children there had had such bad experiences with their fathers, he feared the term would distort their understanding of God. He went on to say that so many of the children there had difficulty giving love to anyone. For most of their lives they had not been loved, so they were incapable of loving. Do you understand? You can't love unless you have been loved. You can't give unless you have first received.

That's why I keep reminding Christians that gathering together for worship and prayer and study and nurture is essential to the Christian life. You cannot live as an authentic Christian out there unless at the same time you are gathering with other Christians to receive all that

God has to give. Our giving will soon exhaust our supply unless we are actively receiving.

I know the truth of that in my experience. Every day I encounter people who are hurting, people with huge needs. I try to be loving and helpful in every way I know how. I give as much as I have to give. But sometimes I get tired. Sometimes I become emotionally drained. Sometimes I become discouraged, and feel that I have nothing left to give. But, almost always, if I am open to it, God will find a way to give me what I need. Sometimes God's help comes through something I am reading. Sometimes God will refresh my spirit through a note from a friend, or a telephone call, or a comment of encouragement. Sometimes it happens in times of prayer. But again and again, often in unlikely ways, I receive from God, and as a result, I am enabled to give.

Of course, to receive from God or from family and friends requires some humility. In order to receive, we must acknowledge that we are not all-sufficient—we need what others can give. But, it is precisely when we become humble enough to receive from God and from others that we are made ready to give to others for the right reason, in the right spirit, and of the right substance. It's just as Jesus said to Peter, "If I do not wash your feet, then you will have no part of me." It's true: unless we receive, we miss out on life as God intends it. Unless we receive, we cannot give. So, for our sakes, we must be willing and able to receive.

II.

There is one more thing we must see. Not only must we receive because we need it. We must also receive because other people need to be able to give.

I love the "Prayer of St. Francis," and especially that phrase, "It is in giving that we receive." Certainly that is true, but the opposite is also true: "It is in receiving that we give."

When we are willing to receive from someone, we are acknowledging that they are persons of worth, and that they have something worth giving to us. So, our receiving is, in reality, giving an important gift to them. Our willingness to receive sets up a two way interchange which makes relationship possible. Every healthy relationship requires both— both giving and receiving from each partner in the relationship.

In some respects, it is easier to give than to receive. It is easier to serve than to be served. If we insist upon always being the giver and never the receiver, it might be because we like to think of ourselves as the superior, self-sufficient person: "I pass out gifts, I don't need them!" You can see, I am sure, how such giving can be a very self-serving, destructive thing. One person is superior, the other inferior. One person has gifts worth giving, the other person has nothing of worth. There can be no real relationship under those circumstances. A healthy relationship requires both giving and receiving from both parties.

With this in mind, take a look at your family, your friends. Are the significant relationships in your life two-way relationships in which all parties give and receive? Or are they relationships in which the same persons always insist upon the giving? This is something we parents need to think about. It is so important to recognize our children and our grandchildren as persons of worth, with very important gifts they can share with us. They have insights. They have feelings. They have experiences to share. If we always insist upon giving without receiving, we are denying them their full humanity, and we are cheating ourselves out of very precious relationships. Once we begin receiving, we may be surprised at how much we have been missing, all because we have refused the gifts of others.

I don't know about you, but I have more difficulty in receiving than in giving. My giving feeds my ego. It makes me feel like a worthwhile person, and there is nothing wrong with that. But what is wrong is that I find it easier to help someone than to receive help from them. I find it very difficult to ask someone to do something for me. I don't know whether I just don't want to impose on them, or whether I feel that I am not worthy of their time and effort, or whether I just don't have enough humility to put myself in a receiving position. I do know that I have difficulty receiving.

But I am working on it, because I know that when I refuse the gifts of others, I am depriving them of something very important to them. And, although I don't intend it, it's really a "put down." I am implying that they don't have anything worth giving to me. And, I know that if I am going to have significant relationships, I must be able to receive as well as give. Here's an important part of that: when you love someone, you want to be able to give to them. But if the one you love thinks that he or she is self-sufficient and has no need of what we have to give, how do we express our love? Don't you see how that gets in the way of relationship? The channel through which love can flow has been cut off. No, there can be no meaningful relationship unless we are able to receive as well as give.

Sometimes, I have done it right. I well remember that when my parents were in their 80's, retired and living on Social Security and a small pension, they never stopped wanting to give to their children as they had done all their lives. So, whenever we would go to see them on vacation, or whenever we had a large expense, my parents would send a check to help out. Now, I could have sent it back, explaining that their retirement income was much smaller than mine and that we could get along quite nicely without their contribution. But that would have been my pride speaking. If I had done that, it would have said to them that they were no longer needed, and it would have deprived them of one of their primary remaining joys—the joy of giving. My willingness to receive from them was one of my best gifts to them. It is blessed to give, that's true; but it's also blessed to receive. That's true too.

Let me say it one more time, and I will close with this. An American woman, Elizabeth Byrd was vacationing in Scotland one year. While traveling through the countryside, she met a local farm woman, a Mrs. McIntosh. Mrs. McIntosh' husband was away at market, and the two women hit it off, so she invited Elizabeth to stay with her overnight. As soon as they arrived at the farm house, it began to rain and the wind began to blow. A storm had come from out of nowhere and it looked like it would be a big one. It wasn't very long before the electricity went out. The two women busied themselves with lighting candles and building a fire in the fireplace. There was a knock at the door, and when Mrs. McIntosh opened it, there was a teen-aged boy from the neighboring farm. He had been born with a deformed leg, and had difficulty getting around. He walked with a serious limp. He explained that his father had tried to call to check up on them, but the telephone lines were down. So, this young man had come to see if they were all right.

The American woman began to talk about how much she liked wind and rain and a roaring fire in the fireplace. "Then, you're not scared?" he asked. Mrs. Byrd started to say, "No, we're not frightened. Everything is just fine!" But, before she could open her mouth, Mrs. McIntosh broke in, saying, "Of course she was scared, and so was I. But now everything is fine. We have a man around!"

The boy broke into a big grin. "I'll see that everything is snug," he said, as he moved toward the door. He felt like he was ten feet tall! He felt very special as he left the farm house that night—all because a very wise Mrs. McIntosh had been willing to receive his gift.

Do you understand? We need to receive, and other people need the experience of giving. It's true, isn't it? As blessed as it is to give, it is also blessed to receive.

Prayer: Father, deliver us from the delusion that we are self-sufficient and have no need of anyone or anything. Help us to receive from You and from others, so that we will have gifts to give. And help us to be able to receive as a very significant way of giving. Hear our prayer of gratitude for Your many gifts of love to us. In Jesus' name we pray. Amen.

24.
Thanksgiving Is a Choice

---

1 Thessalonians 5:15-18

It was a few weeks after the birthday celebration and the mother constantly had been after her 12 year old daughter to write her "thank you" notes. The relationship between them had become quite strained when the girl finally sat down to "do her duty." Her first note was to her aunt who lived out of state. The aunt had sent her a pin cushion, a lovely gift, but not on the request list of many 12 year olds. The note was brief. She wrote: "Dear Aunt Mae, thank you for the pin cushion. It's just what I always wanted—but not very much!"

I suppose the moral to the story is that you can make someone write a "thank you" note. But you can't make them be really thankful. It won't be long before we celebrate Thanksgiving Day. By Presidential proclamation, it will be a day set aside for giving thanks. A President can declare the holiday, but he cannot command gratitude. So, on that day, almost everyone will have a holiday, but not everyone will celebrate Thanksgiving. Probably most will not. But those who do, will do so as a result of a decision. Because, finally, thanksgiving is a choice we make. And that choice has far more to do with the reality inside of us than with the reality around us.

Circumstances do not produce gratitude. They just don't! You know people, as I do, who live in very favorable circumstances, but they are not thankful. Instead, they spend their lives complaining that the good is not better. At the same time, we all know people who have experienced problem after problem, yet they live in perpetual gratitude for the blessings they have received. And they joyfully and expectantly await further expressions of God's love. No, you cannot explain either the presence or the absence of gratitude by looking only at circumstances. Gratitude has far more to do with the inside than with the outside.

Take the Apostle Paul, for example. His was not an easy life. He had been criticized, betrayed, attacked, beaten, stoned, imprisoned, shipwrecked. His "thorn in the flesh" tormented him. And his enemies were such that he lived continuously under the threat of death. If you were looking for external circumstances likely to produce gratitude, you would not choose the circumstances of Paul. And yet, remarkably, his letters are filled with joy and thanksgiving. Again and again he says, "Rejoice in the Lord always." "Thanks be to God." And, as he wrote to the Thessalonians: "Give thanks in all circumstances; for this is the will of God in Christ Jesus for you." From all appearances, his gratitude was in spite of rather than because of his circumstances. But there was something on the inside of him that prompted gratitude.

Of course, we are to give thanks for our obvious blessings. But, according to Paul, our thanksgiving need not be dependent upon our circumstances. He says, "Give thanks in all circumstances!" He is saying that we can decide to give thanks even when in oppressive conditions.

That is exactly what the first celebrants of Thanksgiving did. You know what a rough time they had. A storm at sea blew them off course and they came to the wrong destination. Because of that, the winter was far more severe than they had anticipated. The average food ration got down to five grains of corn per person per day. They began with 102 people in their little colony. Only 50 survived that first winter. Then, they had a choice to make. Either they could gather in bitterness and mourn the tragic reality that half their number had died, or, they could come together in thanksgiving and celebrate the fact that half of them had survived. You know what they chose. And that choice was made not because of something outside of them, but because of something deep within them! They looked for blessings!

I read recently about a man who took a tour of Yellowstone Park and the Grand Tetons. Instead of being impressed with what he saw, at every stop he made a disparaging remark. Nothing impressed him. He was bored by the whole thing. Finally, the tour leader had had enough. He snapped, "Mister, if you haven't got it on the inside, you can't see it on the outside." That's true, isn't it? There are people who can look at a flaming sunset and feel nothing. There are other people who can look at the same sunset and weep for the sheer beauty of it. There are people who can go to a concert to hear the greatest music in the world and fall asleep. And there are others who go to that same concert, sit on the edge of their seats, are moved, and when it is over stand up and cheer. There are people who can sit in the Chapel and be touched and changed by God's grace; at the same time there are people seated side by side with them who are totally unmoved by it all. So much depends upon what you have on the inside!

That's the choice that comes to every person. What do you look for in life? Do you recognize blessings when you see them? Do you believe that every good thing in life comes as a gift from God? Do you see the glass half empty or half full? Do you look for and accentuate the deprivations of life, or the blessings of life? If you don't have the right stuff on the inside, you won't be able to see it on the outside.

I once heard Father John Powell tell a story I have enjoyed. Parents had twin sons who were decidedly different. One was a confirmed pessimist, the other an incurable optimist. The parents worried that each had a distorted view of life. They went to a counselor for help. He said, "I think they can be helped, but the treatment is radical. Christmas will soon be here. On Christmas morning you must provide the best gifts imaginable for the little pessimist. He will have to feel good about it, and he will be cured. But, for the optimist, you must give only a room full of manure. He will not be able to see anything good in that, and he will be cured." So, that is what they did. On Christmas morning, the pessimist looked at his sumptuous gifts and began to whine: "I don't like this. This isn't the right color. This is not what I wanted." But in the other room the optimist was screeching with joy, throwing the manure up in the air and shouting, "You can't fool me. You can't fool me. With all this manure, there has to be a pony in here somewhere!"

Is there any doubt in your mind as to which of the two boys will have the happiest, the most fulfilling life? If you constantly expect the worst, you cannot live the best. You just can't!

Write this down somewhere where you won't forget it, because I'm about to say something important: what you look for in life, you tend to find. We tend not to notice those things we are not looking for. We pass by blessings every day. Even when they are there, we don't see them because our attention is somewhere else. At the same time, we exaggerate our problems and complicate them if we go out looking for them. We sometimes even see problems when they aren't there, if that's what we are looking for.

And, do you know what else? Our expectations help to produce the very things we expect to happen. Psychologists talk about "self fulfilling prophecy:" when we expect something negative to happen, that expectation helps to make it happen. For example, we may expect people to dislike us. We become angry because we don't know why they should dislike us. We begin to resent them for disliking us. Our resentment shows through, and, surely enough, they begin to dislike us! Self fulfilling prophecy! I remember an epitaph a pessimist wrote for his own gravestone. He wrote: "I expected this, and here I am!" It's true. We tend to find what we look for. And our looking for it helps to create it.

I remember my father telling the story of a family moving from one town to another in the horse and buggy days. They loaded all of their possessions onto a wagon and started out. When they came to the outskirts of the new town, they saw one of the locals sitting on a split rail fence, whittling, chewing, and spitting. They pulled their wagon to a stop and called out to the man, "Tell us, what kind of people live in this town?" The man sitting on the fence had a remarkable kind of folk wisdom. Instead of answering the question directly, he asked another question in return. He asked, "What kind of people live in the town you just left?" "Oh," said the man in the wagon, "they were cold, self-centered, un-neighborly." "Well," said the local man, continuing his whittling and spitting, "I imagine you'll find these people to be pretty much the same." The next day another family came to the town and found the same local man sitting on the fence. They asked the same question with the same response, "What kind of people live in the town you just left?" They replied, "They were warm people, friendly people, helpful in every way!" The man on the fence replied, "Well, I imagine you'll find these people to be pretty much the same."

You see, no matter where you go, there is one factor which is constant—YOU! You bring your values, your perceptions, your expectations. And, generally, what you look for, you will find. What you expect to happen, your very expectations will help to make happen. Therefore, happiness and fulfillment in life have far more to do with what you bring than with what you find. That's why it's very practical advice, in the words of the old gospel song, to "count your blessings, name them one by one." Once you start looking for blessings and giving thanks for blessings, that very act helps to multiply the blessings!

The fact is, you cannot always control what life sends your way. And, if you live long enough, you will have your share of disappointment, failure, sickness, and sorrow. That's just the way it is. We cannot control what life sends our way, but we can control what we will do with what life sends our way. It's easy enough to give thanks when life is filled with blessings. And I certainly hope we will do that. But Paul suggests that we Christians have a reason to give thanks even in times of difficulty.

How so? For Paul, the resurrection of Jesus is the keystone of our faith, and the reason for our hope and our joy. Those first century Christians had seen the strong hands of God turn a crucifixion into a resurrection, a defeat into a victory. And, they knew that when they placed themselves into hands as strong as that, they were secure.

That's why they were able to go to their deaths upon crosses or in the torturous arenas of Rome, singing hymns of praise and with smiles of joy and victory on their faces. They knew that God is going to win the final victory, and that they will share in that victory. I tell you, there is no way to defeat a person who really believes that!

Even if we are in difficulty, we are still able to be thankful, because God is here, because He is loving and powerful, because we trust that He is at work in our lives for good, and because we believe that He will win the final victory. And, you know, the more you believe that, the more that very expectation will assist God in making it happen!

In every circumstance, say to yourself again and again: "God is in the business of bringing something good out of the raw material of life." I tell you, if you believe that, nothing can defeat you. And you will have something to be thankful for—in every circumstance of life.

My mother trusted that more strongly than anyone I have ever known. And, because her trust in God was so strong, it produced a quality of life which many people described as "saintly." When mother was ninety-one years of age, living in a nursing home, her husband of seventy years died, and she was very lonely during her last year. She couldn't get around very well, moving only from her bed to a chair with assistance. She was legally blind, seeing only blurs, but unable to read or even to recognize people. She could hear only a little if you would talk loudly into her right ear. I would go to see her, give her a hug, and she would hold me close and say, "Is this my Jim?"

A casual observer might think that she had little to be thankful for, but no one could convince her of that. Her circumstances were deteriorating, and her body was failing her, but there was something positively radiant inside of her, something that produced joy and gratitude. Over the last few years of her life, as her eyesight gradually dimmed, she began to identify with Fanny Crosby, the blind composer of gospel songs. Fanny Crosby was stricken with blindness at six weeks of age. When she was eight years old, she wrote a little poem. My mother memorized it. And, over a period of several months, almost every time I visited my mother, she quoted that poem for me. Listen:

> "O what a happy soul I am, although I cannot see,
> I am resolved that in this world contented I will be;
> How many blessings I enjoy that other people don't!
> To weep and sigh because I'm blind, I cannot, and I won't!"

Isn't that great? My mother learned to give thanks in all circumstances. I visited with her the week before Thanksgiving during that last year of her life. We had a wonderful time together. And before I left, she spoke of her life there at the nursing home. She said, "You know, everyone here is so nice. All my needs are met. And I count my blessings every day!"

Now, remember her condition: blind, deaf, confined, lonely—still, she said, "I count my blessings every day!"

You see, she knew something. She wouldn't be blind forever. She wouldn't be deaf forever. She wouldn't be confined forever. She wouldn't be lonely forever. God would see to it. She knew that. And in the meanwhile, God's grace was sufficient. She knew that too.

You understand, then, what I mean when I say that we Christians are not at the mercy of our circumstances. Thanksgiving does not come from circumstances. Thanksgiving, finally, is a choice!

Prayer: Loving God, our Father, we are grateful for pleasant circumstances in life. Your grace seeks us out, and in so many ways we have been blessed. We pray today for the kind of inner spirit that is not dependent upon favorable surroundings to produce a celebration of thanksgiving. We pray for the kind of spirit that looks for blessings even in the midst of difficulties, and that trusts in your grace even when it is difficult to do so. Make us to know that now and always we are held in your loving and powerful arms. Thank you, Father. In the name of Jesus we pray. Amen.

25.
Lifelong Disciples

Matthew 28:18-20, Hebrews 5:11-6:3 (Phillips paraphrase)

"There is a great deal that we should like to say about this high priesthood, but it is not easy to explain it to you since you seem so slow to grasp spiritual truth. At a time when you should be teaching others, you need teachers yourselves to repeat to you the ABC's of God's revelation to His children. You have become people who need a milk diet and cannot face solid food! For anyone who continues to live on 'milk' is obviously immature—he simply has not grown up. 'Solid food' is only for the adult, that is, for the one who has developed by experience his power to discriminate between what is good and what is bad for him. Let us leave behind the elementary teaching about Christ and go forward to adult understanding. Let us not lay over and over again the foundation truths...No, if God allows, let us go on." (Hebrews 5:11-6:3 Phillips)

People have always attached special meaning to a person's last words. When someone is dying, they don't waste time and energy on the trivial. Whatever a person's last words are, we know they are to taken seriously.

That is why the words from the twenty-eighth chapter of Matthew have always been important to the Church. They are Jesus' last words, and in them he was saying something important to his followers. He told them, and us, what he wants his followers to do, and he assures us that he will be with us as we do it. We call these last words of Jesus "The Great Commission."

According to Jesus, the primary task of the Church is to make disciples, and that is a two part process: first, we are to help people to

be born into the Christian life. That happens through conversion—
that is, being turned around. Turned away from inadequate centers of
meaning, and turned toward the God we have met in Jesus, so that God
becomes the center of our lives, with everything else in life deriving its
meaning and direction from that center. Conversion. We sometimes use
the term, "being saved"—being saved from sin and for the abundant,
God centered life, being saved from meaninglessness for usefulness,
being saved from self-centeredness for God-centeredness. That's what
we mean by being converted, saved, born again. That's the essential
first part of the "making disciples" task.

We hear a great deal about that, especially here in the Bible belt.
But we don't hear nearly enough about the second part of the process.
It is essential to help people be born into the Christian life—that's the
first part. But then after they are born, we are to help people grow up.
The goal is to help people become mature, adult Christians. Both parts
are essential to the Christian life. You can't grow up unless you have
been born; that's true. At the same time, there is something sad about
someone who is born and never grows up.

When Paul wrote his letter to the Hebrews, he had a picture in his
mind of a church filled with spiritual infants, people thirty, fifty, seventy
years old, who still drank from a bottle and who had never begun to eat
solid food. They were people who met regularly to recite their ABC's,
but who had never gone beyond the kindergarten level of the faith. He
said to them, "Let us go forward...to adult understanding." In other
words, "Grow up!"

Of course, learning is an important part of growth. As soon as we
arrive in this world, we begin to learn. We learn from many sources.
The question is: if we want to grow to maturity as Christians, who will be
our teacher? Of course, the answer is: Jesus. That's what it means to be
a "disciple." In the first century, Jesus called 12 people to be disciples—
that is, they were to follow him and to learn from him. Later, they were
called "apostles" because they were sent out to be in mission. But, in the
beginning, they were disciples, followers, learners. And that is what we
are called to be as well—people who learn about life from Jesus.

And, there are two parts to that as well. The Christian faith is an
historic religion. Every thing we believe has its roots in history. There
were some things that God did in history—especially as He acted in
Jesus. So, we are to learn about that. The primary sourcebook is the
Bible. But, of course, even after the canon of the Bible was closed, God
continued to act. So we learn from that as well. All of that is what I
call "the historic word"—all the things that God has done and said
throughout history. That's the first part.

The second part is the context in which we learn about what God has said and done throughout history. Right now, we and all other human beings have questions we are asking, problems we are encountering, experiences we are having. In other words, life is going on. Where Christian discipleship comes alive is at the point of intersection between those two: how what God has said and done in history informs the life we are living right now. So, Christian discipleship is rooted in history, but it is vitally related to what is happening right now. If we only talk about the Bible and Christian history, spend all our time and thought in the first century and before, then the faith is irrelevant. At the same time, if we simply thrash around with the questions we are wrestling with and the problems we are encountering, then we are powerless. But when we get those two together—when we look at the life we are encountering right now in the light of all that God has said and done throughout history, then that's dynamic and exciting and redemptive!

So, to summarize, the task of a Christian disciple is to learn from Jesus, to look at and to live all of life in the light of what God has shown us throughout history, especially in the life, death, and resurrection of Jesus. We are to do that every day for as long as we live, so that we grow and never stop growing, as we become mature, adult Christians. If the right things are happening, as long as you live, you and God will be working on something. If the right things are happening, you are not the same person today that you were a month ago, and you will not be the same person a month from now that you are today. You will be growing, going on to mature, adult discipleship!

All my life I have heard people say or imply that the Church exists primarily for children and youth. I know what they are getting at, because I want nothing but the best for my children and grandchildren too. But, when adults neglect opportunities for their continued growth, when they think they have learned and experienced all they need, and begin to concentrate only on what is available for children, they have it all backwards.

Hear me loud and clear: if you want the best of all possible Christian experiences for your children and grandchildren, with the best of all worlds for them to live in, the place to start is with the adults, because the goal of the Christian faith is to make disciples, mature, adult disciples. And it's impossible to help children grow in that direction unless they have got some samples around. Commercials aren't enough. We need some samples!

That's why, all my adult life, I have invested considerable time and energy in providing opportunities for adult growth, because I know that's where everything good in the Church must start. Isn't it obvious? If we have committed, well-informed adult Christians, then we will have

Church officials who make right decisions; we will have teachers who will teach our children and youth with effectiveness; and we will have parents and grand-parents who will set the right example and provide the right guidance. Unless we have mature, adult Christians, none of those things will happen.

Parents and grand-parents, you have a better opportunity than anyone of helping those in your family to become genuine Christians—but only if you take your faith seriously. You can't pass the faith on to those who come after you, unless you are continuing to grow in faith, not just for their sake, but because that's who you want to be. When children see their parents and their grandparents growing, then their growth is reinforced in the home day in and day out. There are family prayers. They see their parents and grand-parents reading the Bible or other Christian literature. They see their parents and grand-parents being loyal members of the church. They see them becoming more caring about others, more loving, more giving. And they are encouraged to do likewise.

Children are great imitators. There's no doubt about it. They're watching you. And the truth is, we do our most effective teaching when we are least aware of it. One of the greatest fears of my life has been that somehow my example would be a hindrance to my children's Christian faith. For too many children, if they become Christian it will have to be in spite of the example of the adults in their family and not because of it!

What do your children and grandchildren see when they look at you? Do they see an adult who is functioning as an informed and mature person in most parts of your life? Do they see you competent and responsible in your work? Do they see you managing your finances well, keeping up to date and being able to discuss politics, economics, and world affairs in an intelligent way? Taking an interest in your community and investing yourself in organizations and movements that make it a better place?

Do they see all of that, and in contrast, do they see you taking only a marginal interest in your Church, unsure of your beliefs, casual about your faith, and uneasy when you are asked questions about it? If that's the picture your children and grandchildren get, they are probably thinking to themselves, "If it's not important to them, then it's not important to me."

And, you know, they are right, 100% right. If the Christian faith is something primarily for children and youth, something you grow out of, something you don't have to take as seriously later on, then they are right. It's not worth the effort unless it keeps on growing, day after day, as long as we live. It's not worth it unless it takes hold of us as adults and makes an obvious, vital difference in our lives. Our children and youth are watching us, you know. And they are making their decisions about what is important in life. And they are making those decisions not just by what we say, but by what we do.

Tertullian, one of the early Church fathers, said that he and most of the early converts to Christianity were won to Christ not by books or sermons, but by observing how Christians lived and how they died. That's still the way it works.

I admit that I just don't understand those people who say, on the one hand, "I believe in God," but who don't worship regularly, don't take prayer seriously, don't participate in learning and growing opportunities. They say, "I believe in God" but act as if so many other parts of life are more important. They are somehow content to remain spiritual infants. How in the world can you believe in God and not understand that nothing is more important than learning about Him, getting to know Him, learning how more faithfully to serve Him. How can you really believe in God and be casual about it? Most especially, how can you be a parent or grandparent who believes in God and not know the awesome responsibility of that?

Will Durant tells of the time his little girl approached her mother and asked, "Mother, what is God like?" The mother hesitated in the face of so great a question. She could have helped her sew on a button, plan a meal, work a math problem, even talk with her about her boy friend. But, about God she was unsure, so she sent her daughter to her father. The little girl went in to her father and said, "Daddy, what is God like?" He, too, hesitated, unsure of what to say. Later, among her possessions, they found a slip of paper on which she had written a bit of free verse. This what she wrote:

> "I asked my teacher what God is like. She did not know.
> I asked my mother what God is like. She did not know.
> Then I asked my father, who knows more than anyone, what God is like. He did not know.
> I think, if I had lived as long as my teacher, my mother, or my father, I would know something about God."

Of course! They knew so much about the things that were important to them. Tragically, their little girl learned that God was not near the top of their list.

We are called first to be disciples, and then to make disciples. So, every Christian is, simultaneously, both a learner and a teacher. Through the New Testament, we are to live with Jesus every day, listening to him, learning from him. And then, we are to live our lives as his faithful followers, so that all who look at us will know that we are learning from him, that increasingly our lives look and sound like Jesus, and that all of that is of first importance to us. Then, seeing that, seeing the authenticity and meaning of that, they will be called, also, to be his disciples.

If you want that for your life, if you want every day to be growing into mature, adult disciples, there are numerous experiences available to help with that. We have worship times, classes, prayer opportunities, retreat experiences, mission outreaches. You don't have to travel very far to plug in to quality growth experiences.

But it's not going to happen for you and your family unless you make it a priority. You must be ready to say: "This is important. I want to grow up to maturity in Christ. I want to become all that God has created me to be. I'll do whatever is necessary to make that happen."

And, it's not a matter of too little time. Forgive me for being blunt, but that's not a reason; it's an excuse. Each of us is issued the same 24 hours each day. We decide how to invest them. And the fact is, we find a way to take care of that which is important to us. We just do.

And, the good news is that we're not on our own in this. Jesus has promised to be with us and to give us everything we need. I think that's one of the most beautiful promises in all the pages of scripture. Whatever Christ calls us to do, he gives us the grace to do, and he is with us as we do it. He promises, "Remember, I am with you always, even to the end of the world."

Someone has suggested that when we come to the end of our lives and stand before God to give an account of our lives, He will ask but one question. He will ask, "Well, what did you do with it?" What did you do with it? Did you die before you got around to growing up? Or did you become a committed, mature, growing, adult disciple? I know what I want to be able to say!

Prayer: Loving Father, we are grateful that You have created us with such great potential for growth, and that, each day, You call us to come to You, to learn from You, and to stretch out to become the persons You created us to be. Father, do not let us be content with spiritual infancy. Help us to become growing, mature, adult disciples, both for our sake, and for the sake of those we love. In Jesus' name we pray. Amen.

895571

Made in the USA